HOTELS

OF

INDIA

Cheryl Bentley

Hunter Publishing, Inc.
300 Raritan Center Parkway
Edison NJ 08818
(908) 225 1900

ISBN 1-55650-538-8

Published in the UK by:
Bradt Publications
41 Nortoft Rd., Chalfont St. Peter
Bucks. SL9 0LA
England

ISBN (UK only) 0-946983-83-6

Maps by Joyce Huber, PhotoGraphics

Photo Credits
All photographs by author.
Cover photo: Rambagh Palace Hotel, Jaipur

To Don
Whose magic awakened my own

Contents

Introduction

Perhaps we would call their lives ostentatious. They collected women for harems, holidayed around the world, and casually presented jewels as gifts. Their whims were law. The worst of them wasted their money on sex and polo; the best, while guarding a large portion of their wealth for themselves, were conscientious about improving their subjects' lives as well.

India's maharajas have long since marched with the British raj into the country's colorful history. But their world is available to travelers through their palaces, which have been converted to hotels. Scattered throughout India, the hotels offer a glimpse of what life was like when royalty lived in them.

The palace hotels have witnessed much history. Each maharaja had his tale. Many were shrewd rulers, coming from dynasties that had cemented their power through highly practical political means. The Jaipur maharajas, for instance, became vassals of the Mughal emperors during the 16th century, thus ensuring the continuation of their line. The maharajas' last pact was with the British who, in return for their allegiance, allowed them to do as they pleased with their personal lives. Some became no more than caricatures of rulers. One spent a fortune on a wedding for his dogs. Another squirreled away millions of dollars inside his palace, only to forget about it and have the rats eat it up. But the fairy tale ended in 1947 with Indian independence. The princes ceded their kingdoms to the state in exchange for a guaranteed income, the privy purse. However, even this money was later taken away by Indira Gandhi, who had no tolerance for royal perks in a nation of starving people.

The maharajas had to learn to earn a living. With their large staffs and luxurious styles, their palaces were money-losing enterprises. But in 1950 the Kashmir maharaja reversed the trend and converted his palace into a hotel. Other maharajas followed suit. Then more royal family members got into the act, changing smaller homes of wives and relatives into hotels as well. Today India is rich with hotels that were once palaces, hunting lodges, and country homes. Most are in the state of Rajasthan, formerly a warren of principalities, but almost every state has at least one palace hotel. Some of India's finest hotels are former palaces. But the quality of palace hotels varies widely and includes budget inns as well.

The hotels are now playing a role in preserving India's native arts as did their maharajas many years before. Only now the patrons are not the royal family, but tourists who are willing to spend dollars on native crafts.

The hotels come in all prices and styles. Establishments belonging to the Taj, Welcomgroup, and Oberoi chains are luxury hotels. They carry international-class service and prices which, while steep for India, are still below top Western rates. The smaller hotels are often run by royal family members. They lack the gloss of their luxury cousins, but usually have more ambience. Service is almost always courteous, but often laidback and slow. In many you are treated more as part of the family than as a source of rupees. These hotels range from professionally to poorly maintained.

When compared to Western prices, it is downright cheap to sleep like a maharaja in India. Price categories used in this book are (exclusive of taxes and service charges):

Very expensive: $80-$100

Expensive: $40-$80

Moderate: $15-$40

Inexpensive: Less than $15

Prices are for a standard double room. However, tariffs change rapidly and usually go up instead of down. Thus the above prices are only an indication. All rooms are either air-conditioned or air-cooled unless otherwise noted.

To take full advantage of the hotels, guests should be good sleuths. There are many special stories that remain hidden unless you ask. The tiny temple in the courtyard of Udaipur's Lake Palace was the maharaja's. On the edge of the Jai Mahal in Jaipur is Jaipur's first weather observatory, which is unlocked only by request and goes unnoticed by most guests. Usually there is at least one staff member knowledgeable about the hotel's history who will talk with interested guests.

India

Jammu & Kashmir

Himachal Pradesh

Punjab

Haryana ✪ DELHI

Rajasthan

Uttar Pradesh

Sikkim

Gangtok

Arunachal Pradesh

Assam

Nagaland

Meghalaya

Manipur

Bihar

Tripura

Mizoram

West Bengal

Calcutta

Gujarat

Madhya Pradesh

Arabian Sea

Bombay

Maharashtra

Orissa

Bay of Bengal

Andhra Pradesh

Panaji

Goa

Karnataka

Madras

Kerala

Tamil Nadu

Indian Ocean

Trivandrum

SRI LANKA

Royal family members often saunter through their hotels and, depending on their mood, can be responsive to a smile and a request for more information.

Finally, a traveler should leave time for the spaces — gentle moments that evoke the texture of bygone times. Lacy light made by the filigree of carved marble, the mournful wail of peacocks, the windows through which women cut off from all males except their husbands viewed the outside world — all bind the present to the past.

If You Go

It has been said that you either love India or hate it. There is no in-between, perhaps because this is a country of extremes. Spiritual miracles and sleight-of-hand illusions, exquisite architecture and sidewalk hovels, millionaires and beggars, naked holy men and women dripping in jewels, centuries-old erotic temples and modern men who cannot touch women in public all collide, clash, and fuse into new images as part of India's age-old carnival of life.

Confronted by scenes that have scarcely changed for centuries, you feel you are touching the continuity of life in its eternal rhythm of living and dying. Life somehow slows down if you allow it, and you enter into its vast stream. With its brilliant colors, elaborately dressed peasants, pungent spices, and varied handicrafts, India can vie with any country in the world for the Western traveler seeking an entirely different experience.

India bombards your senses. Some travelers retreat to the familiar security of luxury hotels but, to get the most out of this country, you have to accept it on its own terms. Dicker with its auto rickshaw drivers over prices. Talk to some of the people who will surely come up to you wanting to sell everything from rupees to hashish. Visit its temples and try to sense their peace. Be willing to make friends — many Indians are as curious about you as you are about them. Be sensible, but eat the native food. Her fans claim that if you are open, India will leave you different from when you arrived. For those who are willing, a trip through India invariably becomes a journey into self. And what more can real travelers ask?

ENTRY PROCEDURES

Citizens of all countries require visas. Tourist visas are valid for six months. Health certificates are not necessary unless coming from areas infected with yellow fever.

CUSTOMS

200 cigarettes and up to 95 litres of liquor are duty free.

DEPARTURE TAX

300 rupees

CLIMATE

India has three seasons: the monsoon, from June through September; winter, from October through February; and summer, from March until June. The monsoon brings cooling rains, but it can be muggy when it isn't raining. Rains usually come in short showers, but occasionally there are entire days of rain. Winters are delightful with warm days and chilly evenings. Summers are as hot as anyone's vision of hell and surely just as unpleasant. Especially during the summer, and to some extent during the monsoon, fewer tourists are in India. During these times it is easier to find hotel rooms, and some offer low-season discounts.

CURRENCY

Indian money is the rupee. If foreigners don't pay hotel bills with foreign currency or rupees they can prove were received by exchanging foreign money, a hefty luxury tax will be tacked on at better hotels. Be sure to keep all your exchange certificates because if you pay in rupees, hotels usually check to make sure you have exchanged an equivalent amount of foreign currency.

Also, watch out for torn bills. They are not accepted as currency. Indians seem to get rid of their own torn money by passing it on to unsuspecting foreigners. If you are stuck with a torn note, you must go to a bank to have it exchanged for a proper one.

CREDIT CARDS

They are common in the largest cities, less so in provincial areas. To be safe, ask in advance.

HOLIDAYS

There's usually a festival going on somewhere. Since India has a lunar calendar, their dates change annually. Check with the Indian Tourist Office for the exact date. Main festivals include:

Republic Day, January 26. Colorful festivities, especially in Delhi.

Holi, February-March. Everyone has a good old time by throwing colored water and powders on each other.

Sangaur, March-April. Celebrated in Rajasthan.

Teej, July-August. A Rajasthani festival. Jaipur is especially colorful.

Independence Day, August 15. Especially good in Delhi.

Dussehra, September-October.

Diwali, October-November. A festival of lights.

Christmas, December 25. Indians decorate palm and other tropical trees with Christmas glitter.

FOOD

Indian food is characterized by use of such spices as cardamom, coriander, red pepper, and turmeric. It is not all hot or vegetarian. (In fact, the majority of Indians are not vegetarian.) Each region has its own style of cuisine. *Mughlai,* or northern Indian, has many foods cooked in the *tandoor,* a special earthen oven. Foods are often made with a *garam masala* sauce featuring cinnamon, black pepper, cardamom, and cloves. Usually accompanying a meal, yogurt cools and balances spices. Bread is flat, Mideastern in style, and is used to scoop up food in the right hand. (Indians claim eating with the hand enhances the flavor of the food.) South Indian food is hotter, using more coconut and mustard seeds and less oil. Rice is more common than bread. Popular foods include the *dosa,* a crepe filled with potatoes or other vegetables, and *idlis,* rice cakes. Some restaurants feature the cuisine of a special region, but in most places you will find menus with a range of Indian cuisines.

A 20 percent luxury tax is added to restaurant bills in luxury hotels if you pay in rupees. To avoid the tax, use a credit card

With wonderful names like Rosy Pelican, Kingfisher, and Guru, Indian beers are good. Wines are abysmal. You can get foreign wines at luxury hotels, but they are expensive. Safe for drinking, mineral water is commonly available in both restaurants and on the streets.

DRESS

Most people dress informally in India. Women should not wear shorts except in their hotels and in Bombay and Delhi (except Old Delhi), where they are acceptable.

LANGUAGES

Principal languages are Hindi and English. Twelve others are recognized by the constitution. You can almost always find someone who speaks English.

NEWSPAPERS

India has a wealth of English-language dailies. Products of a free press, they are irreverent, spicy, and a great way to learn about the country.

INDIAN TOURIST OFFICES

These government offices are useful for information and brochures:

United States, 30 Rockefeller Plaza, 15 North Mezzanine, New York, NY 10020, tel. (212) 586-4901; 3550 Wilshire Blvd., Los Angeles, CA 90010, tel. (213) 380-8855.

Canada, 60 Blor St. West, Suite No. 1003, Toronto, Ontario M4W 3B8, tel. (416) 962-3787.

United Kingdom, 7 Cork St., London WIX QAB, tel. (01) 437-3677/8.

TRANSPORTATION

Indian Airlines, the domestic airline, is quirky and represents Indian bureaucracy at its worst. It accepts only foreign currency as payment from foreigners.

The Indian railroads are among the world's most extensive. Trains range from the superfast Shatabdi Express with a speed of 140 km per hour to the little blue train to Ooty which goes a mighty 4 km per hour. They are a wonderful way to see and feel the country and to sample Indian life.

Busses are generally crowded and miserable but cheap. Try for deluxe ones if going long distances. At least on these you have an assigned seat.

Cars with driver are available through hotels and tourist offices. Rates are reasonable, and they are often the most convenient way to travel between cities.

Within cities use taxis, auto rickshaws, and rickshaws. Taxis are the most comfortable. Auto rickshaws, sputtering little three-wheelers, and rickshaws are more fun. Use them for short rides. Even though taxis and auto rickshaws are supposed to use meters, they usually don't, so be prepared to bargain.

FOR MORE INFORMATION

Among the most comprehensive guides to India is Lonely Planet's *India*. Other good books are *The Insider's Guide to India* by Kirsten Ellis, *India in Luxury*, Louise Nicholson; and *India* and *Rajasthan* in the Insight Guide series.

Fiction imparting a flavor of India includes *India Gate*, Lacey Fosburgh; *Raj*, Gita Mehta; *Midnight's Children*, Salman Rushdie; and *The Raj Quartet*, Paul Scott. The autobiography of Jaipur's maharani Gayatri Devi, *A Princess Remembers*, is full of fascinating details about court life.

History

Indian history stretches from 3000 B.C., when inhabitants of the Indus River Valley created sophisticated civilizations such as Mohenjodaro and Harappa in Pakistan and Lothal in India.

In 1500 B.C. Aryan invaders from central Asia swept through the country, pushing the dark-skinned native Dravidians to the south. Historians attribute the beginning of the Hindu caste systems to the Aryans, who emphasized such differemces to strengthen their power.

The subcontinent later endured invasions from Greeks, Turks, Huns, and finally, beginning with Babur in the sixteenth century, Muslim Mughals arrived from Afghanistan. The six Mughal emperors (Babur, Humayum, Akbar, Jehangir, Shah Jahan, and Aurangzeb) brought with them a flowering of culture that blended the best of Hinduism and Islam. It was during Shah Jahan's reign in the first half of the seventeenth century that the Taj Mahal was created.

Indians of lower castes often converted to Islam during Mughal rule.

With the decline of the Mughals in the early eighteenth century, the power of the British, who had arrived in India in 1619 to trade, ballooned. By 1850, the British East India Company controlled most of the country.

In 1857 Indians revolted against the British, but fell to superior troops. After the insurgency, the British government formally took over the country.

The English were adept at playing politics with Indian kings, who were allowed to rule their states in return for granting the British certain concessions.

British rule left a legacy of railroads, the English language, and a sophisticated infrastructure.

By 1920, under the leadership of Mahatma Gandhi, the country begain its mostly peaceful battle for independence. Gandhi and such leaders as Jawaharlal Nehru perfected the art of passive resistance through such maneuvers as a strike against the salt tax and peaceful defiance of British laws.

When British rule ended in 1947 thousands of Indians were killed in Hindu-Muslim rioting. The subcontinent was divided at that time into Muslim Pakistan and Hindu India. Mass migrations of Hindus and Muslims occurred, but many Muslims stayed in India.

The 565 kings, or maharajas, who ruled over one-third of India at independence had to decide whether to incorporate their kingdoms into India or Pakistan. They were no longer maharajas, but private (although very rich) citizens.

Jawaharlal Nehru served as India's first prime minister until his death in 1964. In 1966 his daughter Indira Gandhi became prime minister and served until her assassination in 1984. She was succeeded by her son, Rajiv Gandhi, until 1989 when Rajiv's government was swept out of office. During a 1991 comeback attempt, Rajiv was killed by a Tamil liberation terrorist in Tamil Nadu.

Despite such violence, India continues to be the world's largest democracy—clumsy and messy as democracies often are, but with the exception of a few years when Indira Gandhi suspended democratic rights, the country has continually maintained its tradition of freedom.

India is a pluralistic society of approximately 80 percent Hindu, 11 percent Muslim, 2.4 percent Christian, and 2 percent Sikh. Violence between communities makes the news, but by and large India's ethnic and religious groups live together peacefully.

For a more detailed history of India, see *A History of India, Volume One*, Romila Thapar; *A History of India 2*, Percival Spear; *A New History of India*, Stanley Wolpert; *The Peacock Throne*, Waldemar Hansen; *Heir Apparent*, Dr. Karan Singh.

Rajasthan

Women in saris of India's most flaming colors, camel carts, and turbaned men with earrings make this north-western Indian state seem more from *The Arabian Nights* than the twentieth century. Perhaps India's most picturesque region, with a terrain ranging from rolling hills to sand dunes, it is a state more in tune with the age-old tinkle of its womenfolk's chunky silver jewelry than the technological toys of today. Studded with crumbling castles and forts and peopled by a warrior race, Rajasthan is a land of heroes whose lives are still sung by desert bards.

Initiated in earlier times by beheading a buffalo with a single stroke, such heroes are of the Rajput caste. A clan that was already old when the Muslim Mughals conquered it in the sixteenth century, they fought the invaders with great bravery, committing mass suicide in which their women burned themselves to death while the men rode to their final battle dressed in robes of saffron, the color of death. Today in Jodhpur you can still see the handprints of the women before they committed *sati,* self-immolation.

Eventually most of the Rajput kings allied themselves with the Mughals through treaties and, most importantly, marriages. Through the Muslim influence, their women came to be in *purdah,* isolated from all male eyes except their closest relatives. In many palace ho-

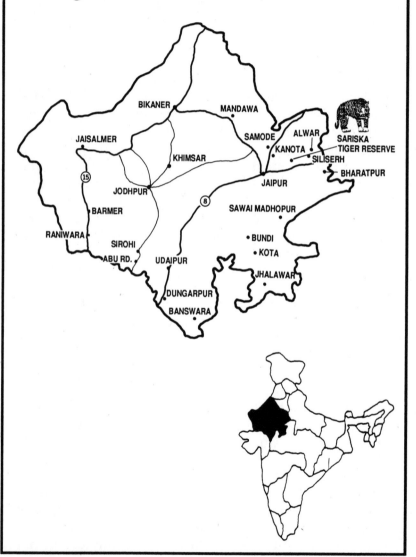

Rajasthan

BIKANER

MANDAWA

JAISALMER

SAMODE

ALWAR

SARISKA
TIGER RESERVE

KANOTA

KHIMSAR

SILISERH

15

BHARATPUR

JODHPUR

JAIPUR

8

BARMER

SAWAI MADHOPUR

RANIWARA

BUNDI

SIROHI

KOTA

ABU RD.

UDAIPUR

JHALAWAR

DUNGARPUR

BANSWARA

tels the *zenana,* or ladies' quarters, from which court ladies watched the passing pageant of the outside world, remains.

In later years the Rajput maharajas became allies of the British, who allowed them to keep their kingdoms in return for their allegiance. It was during the British era that the Rajput princes became a sad parody of their brave ancestors. Instead of spending money on their kingdoms, they frittered it away on women, trips abroad in which they spent lavishly on everything from jewels to Rolls Royces, and hunting parties including up to a thousand servants. But today many of the maharajas have become enterprising businessmen, who will graciously welcome you to their hotels. Most are named Mr. Singh, the Rajput caste name, and are dressed in Western clothes. But if you look closely, you will see the pierced hole in their ears for the earrings of the Rajput male, and the proud stance of a generation of sword carriers.

Jaipur

A city of pink buildings, camels, and crafts ranging from jewelry to rugmaking, Jaipur is one of Rajasthan's most fanciful cities. But in spite of its whimsy this metropolis is no lightweight. Created by a line of crafty rulers adept at playing politics with their sixteenth- and seventeenth-century Mughal conquerors, Jaipur was formerly the richest state in princely Rajasthan and one of the most powerful. Today this city of 1,200,000 serves both as the capital of Rajasthan and as one of the state's most popular tourist destinations.

An exploration of Jaipur should start in the old city, enclosed by massive walls and seven gates. Here there are as many camel carts as cars. Brightly garbed men and women at **Johari, Tripolia, Chandpol,** and **Bapu Bazaars** hawk semi-precious stones, heavy silver jewelry, carpets, miniature paintings, and brilliantly hued textiles.

The **Hawa Mahal,** or Palace of the Winds, lies within the city's heart. This five-story salmon building, adorned with delicate floral motifs, is really just a facade behind which the ladies of the court could gaze at the carnival of life below. Today you can climb to the top and enjoy its panoramic views.

Also in the downtown area is the **City Palace**. A complex built from the eighteenth through the twentieth centuries, the City Palace now houses a fine museum in which you can see lovely, threadbare Persian carpets, finely written manuscripts, swords, and other Jaipur memorabilia. The present maharaja still lives in another part of the palace, and you often find his red-turbaned retainers bustling through courtyards.

The final major site in downtown Jaipur is the observatory, the **Jantar Mantar.** Designed in 1728 by Jai Singh, the maharaja with a scientific bent, the observatory is a series of giant — and still accurate — instruments in surrealistic shapes. Unless you're an astronomer, you probably won't understand the purpose of most of the instruments, but they nevertheless offer a kind of other-wordly experience.

The outstanding Jaipur attraction is located 11 kms outside the city. Begun in 1592, the palace complex called **Amber** sits on its own hill overlooking a lake. It offers fine examples of Rajasthani architecture. Especially notable is the hall of mirrors, a room covered with tiny pieces of mirror. A palace employee will light a candle here, making the room seem like a magical sky lit by a thousand stars.

Hotel Bissau Palace

If your pocket is not running over with rupees, but you want a taste of the royal life, the Hotel Bissau Palace is for you. This hotel combines moderate rates with a delightful clutter of Rajasthani memorabilia. In addition, it packs such extras as a garden with rich bird life, a small pool, and tennis courts.

The feeling here is of living the leisurely life of landed lords and ladies. The wooden-floored lounge is the kind of room you might have seen in your grandmother's old photos. Red lamp shades with tassels crown brass lamps. A painting of the maharaja of Bissau surrounded by his nobles hangs over the fireplace. Swords which were actually used in skirmishes against the Muslims adorn the walls.

A small library opens off the sitting room. Its dusty display cases are cluttered with heavy Rajasthani jewelry, weapons, vases, and photos ranging from a tiger hunt to Lord Mountbatten visiting the Bissau family. The books are of another era. Titles include *Heraldry for Craftsmen and Designers,* Roland Ward's *Record of Big Game,* and *The Glories of Hindustan.*

Built in 1919, the hotel perfectly captures the faded opulence of its days as the town house of the maharaja of Bissau, a village 200 miles northwest of Jaipur. Since Bissau was one of the smaller territories under Jaipur, the Bissau maharaja often came to Jaipur on business and stayed here. Before it was converted to a hotel in 1977, such luminaries as Princess Margaret and a British high commissioner stayed at the Bissau. Today the hotel is run by the last maharaja's son, who lives upstairs. He and his sons keep a low profile, but they can often be seen sipping drinks in the lobby.

The six singles here are in a nearby guest house. While cheap, they are tiny with little charm. Best bets are the 18 doubles and suites. They come with the maharaja's wooden furniture, which has an appropriately faded look. Number 10, one of the nicest doubles, has Rajasthan brass lamps. Swords and shields surmount the bed. The bath boasts an antique tub along with a modern sink. Number 5 is also a double with ambience. Suites ($25) consist of bedroom, small sitting room, dressing room, and bath. The hotel has 24-hour room service, a bar, restaurant, and library. All singles are air-cooled; other rooms are air conditioned.

Outside Chandpole, Jaipur 302 016, Rajasthan, India. Telephone (0141)74191. Telex 365-2644 REGI-IN. AE, MC, V. Inexpensive.

Jai Mahal Palace Hotel

For most of its life the Jai Mahal has been the cast-off stepsister of the Jaipur palace family. With a colorless past as forgotten royal property, the structure was mostly ignored in its 200-year history. It had given way to cobwebs and peeling paint when it was rescued in 1984 by the Taj Group. Taj kept its core but decked it out with a fanciful exterior of cupolas and arches and a new wing.

Today the two-story, 120-room hotel lives a double life. At times it so brims over with tour groups that it could be any modern, luxury hotel. But catch it in its stillness between tour groups, and it will whisper of an age which courted Beauty for no other reason, you suspect, than that it loved her deeply. The hotel gently leads the twentieth-century eye back to spaces full of arabesques, curves, and playful embellishment. Here stone is chiseled like fine lace. Light from filigreed lamps dances delicately on ceilings. Peacocks strut in Persian gardens.

Those gardens are among the Jai Mahal's outstanding features. Designed by Elizabeth Moynihan, wife of U. S. Senator Moynihan, they are a replica of gardens in the Indian city of Dholpur made by the Mughal emperor Babur in 1525. The garden is on different levels to encourage water flow. The pond closest to the hotel symbolizes a half-open lotus, the second, a lotus in full bloom, and the third is the dying flower. On the fourth pond is a platform on which dancers would have performed in Babur's time.

It is appropriate that gardens should be one of the hotel's best features, since the property entered the royal line as a garden. Its first recorded owner was a Mr. Natani in 1720, an influential advisor to Maharaja Jai Singh, the founder of Jaipur and the creator of the observatory Jantar Mantar. Whether there was a structure here is unclear, but the property, known as Natani Ke Bagh, had celebrated gardens.

Today there are two small stone pillars at the foot of the garden near the fourth pond that perhaps date from that period. They are imprinted with what is said to have been deities of the Natani family that originally came from the Indian state of Gujarat. The outlines of the gods carved at their heads have now grown faint with time, but their power, a gentle one from having looked at life for over three centuries, remains.

During British times the property became the official residence of the Resident Surgeon. Dr. T. H. Hendly, who later wrote *Rulers and Chieftans of Rajasthan,* stayed here. Then it became the official residence of the dewans (prime ministers) of Jaipur state. The last dewan to live here in 1940 was Sir Mirza Ismail, whose name is on one of Jaipur's largest streets. In 1950 it was renamed Jai Mahal and converted into a hotel, which by all accounts was abysmally run by royal family employees. Today it is owned by Jagat Singh, the youngest son of the last maharaja, Man Singh. It is, however, leased to the Taj chain and bears the fine decor and efficient service characteristic of that organization.

History buffs might want to check out the 1880 weather observatory at the back of the hotel grounds. The bottom floor is currently used as a room for visiting Taj employees, but the winding staircase up two stories past the skeletons of ancient weather instruments tell an old story. Other than the employee room, the observatory has remained virtually untouched for a century.

In addition, the top floor provides good views of the hotel grounds. The hotel does not encourage visits to the observatory, but a polite request will provide an escort and a key to unlock the door.

The Jai Mahal itself is more a product of modern times. Almost completely rebuilt by the Taj using marble and native Rajasthani stone, it includes only a fraction of the original. One of the domes over the lobby is from the old building, as is the small building, formerly a guest house, to the side of the lobby. Room numbers 266 and 366 were part of the original palace. In addition, the marble in the second floor terrace comes from maharaja times.

All the hotel's standard rooms are similar, in greens, blues, or browns. Bed-sitting rooms are slightly larger than regulars with a larger sofa and a refrigerator. Chairs and headboards are in *jalli,* the Rajasthani crisscrossed style. Rooms are decorated with prints of architectural drawings, showing Indian palaces and museums. Baths in rooms over the lobby have white marble. Other baths have polished granite floors with white-tiled walls.

The lobby features a coffered ceiling and furniture with Indian-style bolsters. The fine court-style paintings found throughout the hotel are the work of local painters commissioned by the Taj group.

The Jai Mahal also has a lawn overlooking the gardens on which guests can sip drinks, watch nightly puppet shows or take sunrise lessons from the house yoga teacher. In the corner of the yard is a giant chess set with elephants, camels, and horses as pieces. Mughal emperors used to while away their days directing servants to move pieces on similar giant boards.

The Jai Mahal offers a restaurant and a bar. It does not have physical fitness facilities at present, but joggers will find plenty of space in its 20 acres and guests can use the health club and pool of its sister hotel, the Taj-owned Rambagh Palace.

Jacob Road, Civil Lines, Jaipur 302 006, Rajasthan, India. Tel. (0141)68381, India; 1-800-ILUVTAJ, United States; (01)828-5909, United Kingdom. Telex 365 2250 JMPH IN. 365 2716 TAJJ IN. Fax (0141)68337. Very expensive.

Mandawa House

This rectangular, two-story structure is the newest of Jaipur's palace-hotels. Owned by the same family who run Castle Mandawa in Mandawa, it was made into a hotel in 1989.

The squared-off edges of its walls set the tone for Mandawa. Although it has the arches, ancestral pictures, and display of weapons found in other palace hotels, there is something modern about this hotel. The Mandawa is an excellent choice for travelers seeking a moderately-priced establishment with both up-to-date rooms and a bit of history. Its 18 standard rooms all have new decor. In addition, you don't feel you are sleeping with the dust of the ages here. It is as spotlessly clean as a five-star hotel.

The building was constructed in 1896 by Bhagwat Singh, whose picture hangs in the dining room. The Singh family had ruled Mandawa since 1730, but they were also under Jaipur's protection and needed a place to stay when in that city on business. Devi Singh, father of the four sons who now manage the hotels, lived here in 1952 when he was elected to the Rajasthan Assembly as a member of the conservative Swatantra Party. Today Singh lives at Mandawa House and is one of its charms. You see him frequently sitting on the terrace reading, a 68-year-old gentlemen with enormous moustaches. He is a repository of family history and would be open to a request by a respectful guest to share his knowledge.

Of interest to the historically-minded are a painting of Sheakaeha, the thirteenth-century ancestor who began the family's rule when he was given 300 villages in what is now known as the Shekhawati region, where Mandawa Castle is located. Also note a shield made of rhino skin and 400-year-old armor.

Rooms are small. All are air conditioned. Beds with bright bed spreads in Rajasthani fabrics are on platforms. There is no bar, but you can get beer here. However, on occasion the staff has to go to the store for it, so be prepared for a long wait.

Sansar Chandra Road, Jaipur 302 001, Rajasthan, India. Tel. (0141)75358. Telex 365 2342 CMDW IN. V. Low season rates available if you negotiate when registering. Moderate.

Narain Niwas Palace Hotel

When the Narain Niwas was built in 1881, it was surrounded by forest. Tigers came frequently to drink water. Panthers arrived to eat the many peacocks strolling around the grounds. It was the garden house built by Narain Singhji, a Rajput chieftan from Kanota, an area 15 km from Jaipur. A vassal of the Jaipur maharaja, Singh stayed here when in Jaipur. The Narain Niwas is appropriately close to Rambagh Palace. But by 1957 the forest had disappeared. With the change in family fortunes the Narain Niwas was opened as a hotel in 1978. Only the peacocks still strolling around its grounds hark back to formerly wild times. Today the hotel remains very much as it was. Two wings, depending on the light, sometimes golden, sometimes pink, with scalloped Mughul arches, flank a central section. The wings are capped by two three-story towers. A cannon rests in front. The property is surrounded by gardens.

Those who enjoy hotels fitting comfortably into the previous century will like this one. Throughout the building you find original frescoes, with paint made from crushed semi-precious stones, bordering arches and defining pillars. The Narain combines a happy collection of nineteenth-century East India Company furniture with Afghan carpets, Rajasthani swords and shields, and native *sanganeri* (hand block) curtains. The dining room/lobby sports dark wood furniture with elaborate carving, lots of arches, and pink pillars. As in

Ceremonial elephant, Jaipur

Amber, Jaipur

Entering Amber (left)   *Narain Niwas Palace Hotel, Jaipur*

Samode Palace Lobby

Samode Palace, Samode   *Rajasthan native (right)*

most palace hotels, paintings of ancestors preside over the room. All 22 rooms are different. All have 17-ft-high ceilings. At slightly higher prices ($28) are deluxe doubles, numbers 21-24. The centerpiece of 21 is the red and maroon marble fireplace. The room comes with gold wicker furniture, chandelier, and a pink marble table with ornate legs that definitely is from times with a taste for embellishment. Number 22 is the hotel's best, with frescoes and red-velvet furniture sporting carved wooden legs. Number 23 is especially large. It has an interesting tall wooden dresser. Upholstery on an ancient sofa is floral. Frescoes surmount the fireplaces. Number 24 also has frescoes and a fireplace. The furniture is gold wicker. Standard doubles contain four-poster beds and also have frescoes. Numbers 33-36 are the best standards. Mohan Singh, grandson of the Narain's founder, runs the hotel. He is often seen lounging on the verandah. Although willing to answer guests' questions regarding the hotel's history, he seems to lack the gift of gab and needs considerable probing to get him to talk.

Kanota Bagh, Narain Singh Road, Jaipur 302 004, Rajasthan, India. Tel. (0141)563448. Telex 0365 2482 NNPH-IN. AE, DC, MC, V. Special rates negotiable during low season. Moderate.

Raj Mahal Palace Hotel

Although leased by the Taj group, this small ivory hotel with a wide stretch of lawn lacks the high gloss marking Taj hotels. Which is part of its charm. From the maha-

Samode House, Jaipur

raja's massive, unrestored wooden furniture to the dust on the polo trophies in the display case, the clock has stopped somewhere in the 1950's for the Raj Mahal. If you are of a romantic bent, charmed rather than bothered by a genteel, crumbling ambience, this ll-room hotel is for you.

Owned by Bhawani Singh, Jaipur's current maharaja, the Raj Mahal has been in suspended animation for years while Singh and the Taj group negotiate its future. It could be renovated at any minute, but given the relaxed Indian concept of time, it could also continue as is for years.

Built approximately 250 years ago by Maharaja Jai Singh for one of his wives, the Raj Mahal was used during the Raj as a British Residency. With Indian independence in 1947, Maharaja Man Singh claimed the property. It was a guest house for his daughter's wedding, which was listed in the *Guinness Book of World Records* as the most expensive wedding in the world. After Rambagh became a hotel, Singh and wife Gayatri Devi moved here where they continued their bustling social life. Jacqueline Kennedy stayed here as their guest.

The hotel is still marked with reminders of Man Singh's stay. Display cases are crammed with polo trophies he won and black-and-white photos marking key events. One picture taken in 1935 entitled "Gathering of Famous Polo Players," shows the darkly handsome maharaja. Another "Exhibition Polo Match," in honor of Mrs. Kennedy in 1962, features Devi.

The lounge, the couple's library, has heavy furniture in Burmese teak, the Rolls Royce of the teak world. The dining room includes a painting of Man Singh and a working fireplace.

No two of the 11 rooms are alike. All are huge. Of the doubles, numbers 1 and 7 are the best. Number 1 has a Burmese teak fireplace, scruffy curtains said to be from the original palace era, a chandelier, and a bath as large as most hotel rooms. The bathroom has an antique marble tub. Number 7 is even larger, with arches and old furniture, a large dressing room, and a terrace with marble columns.

Suites ($150) are the size of city apartments. The doors in the Maharaja Suite still have their original gold-work. Oriental carpets are threadbare. It also features a terrace, dressing room, dining room, and pink marble bath. The Maharani Suite, sparsely furnished for its size, has a sitting room, bedroom with a painting of a nude woman, and pink-and-white-marble bathroom.

One of Raj Mahal's most charming features is its mar-ble-columned terrace overlooking both the lawn and a small swimming pool, which often does not contain water. Here you can sip your drink seated at old-fash-ioned tables. The hotel also includes a bar. The office of the present maharaja is in the back of the hotel. It, too, is in its own time warp with ancient typewriters, desks stacked high with papers, and two elderly male secre-taries. The maharaja comes briefly to the office every day when he is in town.

Sardar Patel Marg, Jaipur 302 001, Rajasthan, India. Tel. (0141)61257-9, India; 1-800-ILUVTAJ, United

*States; (01)828-5909, United Kingdom. Telex 0365-313
JAI IN. Fax c/o (0141)73798. AE, DC, MC, V. Expensive.*

The Rambagh Palace

Their world was one of jewels, polo matches, and hobnobbing with the likes of Queen Elizabeth and Jacqueline Kennedy. But Rambagh always called Maharaja Man Singh and his beautiful wife Gayatri Devi back. Although Man Singh's first and second wives also lived here, Rambagh was the maharaja's special retreat with Devi. He remodeled and gave his own quarters to his young bride. They were in the outer palace, far from the *zenana,* the women's quarters where wives number one and two lived. While Devi had to be in seclusion, or *purdah,* when appearing in public elsewhere in conservative Jaipur, at Rambagh the European-educated maharani could be free. When compared to court life at the City Palace, Rambagh was informal, offering the couple a semblance of normal life. Marriages to his first two wives had been political, but Man Singh's and Devi's was a union of love which would last until his death in 1970.

Their pleasure palace began as a garden lodge in the nineteenth century, built by a lady in the queen's court who created a profusion of flowers, trees, and pools in what had been a wilderness of wild animals and parched earth.

In the late nineteenth century Maharaja Sawai Ram Singh II converted the gardens into a hunting lodge with the help of Sir Swinton Jacob, designer of Kota and

Bikaner palaces. The present dining room and the seven rooms above it are the site of the original building. It later became known for its gardens, which are still lush. Man Singh enlarged the palace in 1931 and made it his official residence. But in 1958 over Devi's objections the maharaja turned his palace into a hotel. Members of his family took turns at running it until the seventies, when it was leased to the Taj chain, which still manages it.

Probably more than in any of India's palace hotels, you can still feel the spirits of its last occupants here. With polo sticks on the walls and a lovely fountain with mosaic floor, the Polo Bar was created in honor of the polo-loving Man Singh, who, in fact, died while participating in a polo match.

His widow lives close to the Rambagh and often appears in the dining room, the Suvarna Mahal, and the Polo Bar entertaining guests. She is still treated like royalty by an indulgent staff who ignore such quirks as when Devi recently threw a party at the hotel but insisted that all guests bring their own booze. "More people than ever showed up," laughs one employee, "because everyone wanted to show they weren't too cheap to furnish their own liquor."

She and Bhawani Singh, son of the last maharaja by another wife, are feuding over property rights. Man Singh's other sons, Pat, Joey, and Jagat, are lined up with Devi against Bhawani, who is better known by his nickname "Bubbles" because of the prodigious amounts of champagne drunk to celebrate the birth of this male heir. The Rambagh staff worries over the royal feud as they would members of their own family. "So sad," murmurs one. "They're all of the same family."

But the Rambagh has reminders of the family in gentler times. Near the Polo Bar is the *zenana* porch where Man Singh's first two wives lived. You can still see the Italian marble staircase which was the separate entry to the *zenana*. Most suites here are in the *zenana*. The four Royal Suites ($510) are works of art. The Maharaja and Maharani Suites were formerly the apartments of Gayatri Devi and Man Singh. The two Maharaja Suites are in Victorian decor with canopied beds. The black and white marble bath in the Maharaja Suite number 221 was designed by Devi. The Maharani Suite with typical Rajasthani decor was her main bedroom. This one has a shower with water coming from all sides as well as the top. The Princess Suite is perhaps the most striking of the Royal Suites. With a dramatic black and white marble floor, chunky-legged Indian-style furniture, and a mosaic-floored fountain, the suite has its own terrace and private garden.

Less elegant, but notable historically, are the deluxe suites ($250), the PinkRose and the Peacock Suites, which were part of the second wife's quarters. The PinkRose includes a large, high-ceilinged bedroom, dressing rooms, and spacious marble bath. The Peacock Suite is adorned, appropriately enough, with a peacock in mirror work on the wall. It has a large bathroom and an exercycle.

At higher prices are the luxury suites ($320). Outstanding ones include the Pushp Niwas, a huge room with living and dining space and beautiful views of gardens and strolling peacocks; and the Pothikhana Suite, once the maharaja's library, and now a spacious living/bedroom, dressing room, and bath.

All standard rooms are furnished in international luxury hotel style. Rooms 101-124 have perhaps the lowliest origins as former service and linen rooms.

The Suvarna Mahal, the dining room, is where Devi and her husband entertained guests. It still carries much of the overblown elegance characteristic of Indian royal taste. You enter through massive wood doors into a room with curved ceiling and three chandeliers. The ceiling is painted with cameos of a blue sky and classical Greek women — the whole edged in gilt molding. The ceiling and a 130-year-old piano are from palace times. The high-backed turquoise and gold chairs and the gold and ivory silk-covered walls have been added by the hotel.

For the health-minded the Rambagh has a health club, squash, tennis, and badminton courts, and an indoor pool. During the hotel's early days, Devi posted her maid at the pool to ward off guests while she had her morning swim.

It is perhaps while sitting on the terrace that you can best sense the hotel's royal heart. Four stone lions stand guard at the terrace's edge. Beyond lies an expanse of lawn marked by magenta bougainvillea. In the distance is Moti Doongri, the fort on top of its own hill. During palace days Devi admired Moti Doongri. Her husband promptly gave it to her.

Along with the views, the Rambagh also surrounds you with a playful interplay of styles. There is a sweep of

curved and straight edges. Door frames are carved marble. Some arched windows are adorned with lattice
work; others have plants spilling from them. At night
lamps make lacy light on the ceiling. Here you feel very
close to Man Singh and Gayatri Devi, the couple who
always returned to Rambagh.

*Bhawani Singh Road, Jaipur 302 005, Rajasthan, In-
dia. Tel. (0141)75141, India; 1-800-ILUVTAJ, United
States; (01)828-5909, United Kingdom. Telex 3652254
RBAG IN, 3652147 RBAG IN. Fax (0141) 73798. AE, D,
MC, V. Very expensive.*

Samode House

A plainer version of its sister hotel the Samode Palace,
this 150-year-old building nevertheless has the best
maintained and most authentically furnished rooms of
any of Jaipur's moderately priced palace hotels. Here
not only suites, but also standard rooms, come equipped
with ambience.

A rambling four stories with most of the 20 hotel rooms
around a central courtyard, the Samode was originally
the *haveli,* or town house, built 150 years ago by Rawal
Sheo Singhji, a prime minister in the Jaipur court.
Members of the Singh family have occupied the home
ever since. Today Raghvendra Singh, along with
brother Yadvendra, runs this hotel and the one in
Samode. He lives with his family in an upstairs apartment. The young brothers have little contact with
guests.

Raghvendra says that as a child growing up here, he was taught that he was in a special place of beauty. Indeed, Samode has some of the most interesting and best maintained treasures of any palace hotel. With native art filling entire rooms and fine antiques in hidden corners, it is a hotel that delights the eye.

Its dining room with arches and pillars is a bouquet of frescoes. Paintings with bright geometric and floral designs are on every inch of free space. These, as well as the frescoes at the entrance, are the original 150-year-old ones. There are frescoes on the patio as well, flowers with a pastel blue background. These, however, have been redone, following the original design. Also unique are the patio floor's tiles in colorful designs. They, too, date from the building's construction.

But the main attractions surely are its two suites. Suite number 115 was formerly the apartment of the Singh brothers' mother. Walls and ceilings abound with pieces of mirror, along with frescoes of flowers and scenes from court life. The room's arches are crowned with mirrors. Pillars have gold and blue frescoes. In the bathroom a 150-year-old fresco rests over a 1980s tub.

Suite number 114 is a room of mirrors, painted columns, and colored glass windows (another Rajasthani craft). A large painting has a scene from the Indian god Krishna's life. This suite has fine city views. It was formerly a terrace, then a chamber for ladies.

All large doubles have arched-ceilinged platforms. Here you sit on cushions and look out the windows. They contain pieces of furniture from the family's collection. But unlike original furniture found in many palace hotels, the furniture here has been well maintained.

Although all rooms have a Rajasthani charm, number 109 is the nicest. It has frescoes of court life over the bed, a large dressing room, and a roomy bath.

As yet the Samode has no bar, though one is planned.

Gangapole, Jaipur 302 002, Rajasthan, India. Tel. (0141)42407. No credit cards. Moderate.

PUSHPENDRA SINGH KAMA

Pushpendra Singh has witnessed two revolutions. One saw Jaipur abandon its monarchy for a democracy. The other was with his own identity. In his 54 years Singh has moved from being an aristocratic Rajput (Rajasthan's ruling caste) to a struggling member of the middle class. He has gone from driving a car to getting around on a motorcycle. He has seen his wife in *purdah,* isolated from most males, and his daughters become an assistant professor and a medical doctor.

Most appropriately, much of the drama of Singh's life was played out at the Rambagh, which has undergone its own revolution as it moved from palace to hotel. Now purchasing manager, Singh joined the Rambagh in 1962. He felt at home at the hotel since he was related to the Jaipur maharaja. Many generations ago, as a younger son, Singh's ancestor was given land while his older brother was made maharaja. Today Singh is twelfth in line to the throne.

Had his grandfather not lost most of his estate in 1953 to a government land-distribution program, Singh would have followed the family tradition of managing their property, or perhaps a career in the military. But changing times forced him to scramble for another career. In 1962 Jai (Joey) Singh, younger son of Maharaja Man Singh, was running the Rambagh. Singh turned to his relative for a job.

The Rambagh, he remembers, was very different from the luxury hotel it is now. It had not then been extensively renovated. "Today you find false ceilings," he says. "Then the ceilings were very high." They also did not have air conditioning. Rooms were cooled as they had been since 1932 with fans blowing cool breezes from wetted mats. A double room with all meals went for approximately $13.

Instead of having benefits, employees relied on Joey's largesse. "He was very generous in looking after the staff's welfare," recalls Singh. "He was aware of families. On his own he would give monetary help. That is very rare with the new generation."

In 1972 the Taj Hotels leased the Rambagh. The mild-mannered Rajput remembers that they "raised rates, renovated, brought the hotel to international standards." Taj also raised employees' salaries and gave them pension and health benefits.

Those were the days of the Vietnam War when nurses and soldiers often stayed at the Rambagh. Working at the reception desk until 1972, Singh enjoyed meeting foreigners and learning about their way of life. "Before, I would have found out about them only through books," he says. He also delighted in their reactions to India. "Many thought of our country as one of only snake charmers. Which it was not."

Working at the hotel, he says, educated him, making him want to give his daughters the highest education possible. "We used to believe in early marriage," he explains. "Education for women was for pastime only." His wife observed *purdah* with her in-laws, but later discontinued the custom with everyone except his father, who is horrified at the independence of the women in Singh's family.

Singh pauses. He says softly that his father is "impossible. He is confined to his own house. He longs for the past." But Pushpendra Singh has no nostalgia for a way of life that has misted away with the modern age. "I think I have changed according to the time," he says proudly.

Kanota

A small village some 20 minutes from Jaipur, Kanota is a good place to sense the life of land-owning nobles without foregoing civilization.

Kanota Castle

This two-story structure of beige stone sits securely behind the ramparts of its 200-year-old fort. Perhaps the nearby Shiva temple has blessed both castle and fort, for their owners have never had to defend this postage- stamp-sized territory.

In 1990, four generations after its founding, the castle began another phase of its life as owner Mohan Singh turned it into a 35-room hotel.

Belonging to the owners of Jaipur's Narain Niwas, the Kanota features frescoes painted with crushed semiprecious stones in its lobby, along with a hodge-podge of Victorian furniture, a billiard table and, of course, a stuffed tiger. More soothing is the long verandah, its path of arches decorated along the top with paintings. Here you can sit and imbibe the aura of this desert fort.

Rooms contain the palace's collection of elderly furniture. Worthy of note are the windows of Rajasthani-style colored glass. As yet there is no air conditioning in the palace, but a system is in the planning stages.

Narain Niwas Palace Hotel, Kanota Bagh, Narain Singh Road, Jaipur 302 004, Rajasthan, India. Tel. (0141) 563448. Telex 0365 2482 NNPH IN. AE, DC, MC, V. Moderate.

Samode

The only reason anyone comes to this tiny village 40 km from Jaipur is to see Samode Palace. The area also offers glimpses of rural life, with villagers' brilliantly colored garments brightening the desert brown.

Samode Palace

Rawal Singh loved to spend money. It is said this nineteenth-century chief minister of Jaipur exhausted state funds. No one knows if those monies were diverted to his palace in the small village of Samode, some 40 km from Jaipur. But even if the palace grew from less-than-honest funds, the results of Singh's efforts are a jewel box of a palace hotel.

Here the creators of Samode — many generations added to the palace — pushed craftsmanship to its limits, magically stopping before their efforts became ostentatious. At this golden-hued palace art cuts through the differences in generational styles, speaking to the individual's appreciation of the beautiful.

Rawal's own creation, the Sheesh Mahal, or the Hall of Mirrors, is one of a number of halls completely covered by pattern, from walls punctuated by Rajasthani arcades of arches fastened by fluted marble columns, to ceilings, with pattern upon pattern, colors and textures juxtaposing and blending. Floral and geometric arrangements are interspersed with larger paintings of court life. In the Sheesh Mahal the designs are in *meenakari,* the native form of enameling, and studded with pieces of mirror. Other walls and ceilings are decorated in frescoes. Each hall is a work of art, beckoning the viewer both to delve into the room's garden of forms and to stand back and appreciate the overall effect. So completely does the palace weave a spell from times long past that it might be from a fairy tale. In fact, Hollywood has discovered its charm. *The Far Pavilions* was filmed here, as have been numerous Hindi movies.

The 32 rooms and suites also reflect their lavish Rajasthani past. Surrounding a central courtyard, they include the family's nicely maintained old furnishings and paintings of ancestors. Many rooms have four-poster beds and pillows for lounging under Mughul arches.

Samode Palace is owned and run by Raghvendra and Yadvendra Singh, descendants of the family who built it. The family still has connections to the village of Samode. When a Singh son gets married, he meets Samode's citizens in what Raghvendra calls a "fascinating, non-ending procession." He then spends the night with his new wife in the village. In addition, the entire family congregates at the palace during the festivals of Gangaur in March-April (the Hindu calendar changes yearly); Dussehra in September-October; and Diwali in October-November. Since villagars participate, this is a particularly colorful time to visit Samode.

Samode 303806, District Jaipur, Rajasthan, India. Tel. (0141) 42407. No credit cards. Moderate.

Alwar

Life here is definitely away from the fast lane. This northeastern Rajasthan city allows you to kick back and soak up the sites of an area still largely unaffected by tourists. People here are genuinely friendly and curious about foreigners. Expect a few childlike stares. Even auto rickshaw drivers don't inflate their prices upon seeing a light skin. However, for the inveterate sightseer Alwar offers the crumbling **Bala Quila Fort**, still guarding the city from its hilltop home, and the museum in the palace — now a government agency — displays miniature paintings and weapons.

Lake Palace Hotel

One hundred eighty-three years ago a dark-eyed Rajput beauty named Sili captured the heart of maharaja Vinay Singh. But Sili was loyal to her village nestled in a cup of hills near a lake 20 km from Alwar. Not even the luxuries of Alwar could lure her away. And so Vinay brought the court to Sili. Building a five-story structure stepped up a hill opposite a lake, he used the palace for a weekend retreat. Subsequent maharajas employed it as a hunting lodge. Eventually the State of Rajasthan took over the property and turned it into a government-owned Rajasthan Tourist Development Corp. hotel in 1980.

Although large and rambling, the yellow plaster Siliserh (or Lake Palace) lacks the flamboyance of most of its royal cousins. Its drama stems from the lake, half-dry during the summer, full during the monsoon. With its many terraces bringing the out-of-doors to the palace, this is a place for nature lovers.

Of its 11 rooms, six are air-cooled. Three doubles and two singles have fans only. Air-cooled doubles 101 and 104 have lake views. Number 104's centerpiece is its circular bed platform in the room's center. Air-cooled doubles 201-205 are similarly furnished with native rugs and marble-topped tables. They share a common lounge with TV. The top floor's three double rooms have entrance hall, vaulted ceiling, and tiny alcove with stained glass windows. These rooms open on to a terrace with beautiful views of the lake and hills. The small singles include lake views.

Furniture in the dining room is threadbare, but the room's many windows and terraces draw the eye outdoors and away from the restaurant's poor maintenance. The hotel also has a bar and can arrange boating trips.

Lake Palace, Siliserh, District Alwar 301 001, Rajasthan, India. Tel. 22991. No credit cards. April-July 25% discount. Inexpensive.

Phool Bagh Palace Hotel

This run-down old former royal guest house has seen tragedy. Built in 1935 by the Alwar maharaja to house Indian princes for a coronation, the palace remained unused until Pratap Singh, the maharaja's elder son, lived in it with his wife and two children from 1959-77. The family occupied 70 acres of gardens, farmland, and horse and elephant stables. The animal-loving young wife, Mahendra Kumari, kept many pets here ranging from dogs to a young lion. However, family life ended in 1977 when the anti-royal Indira Gandhi began jailing royals. Upon hearing that he was to be arrested, Pratap claimed it was not fitting for a proud Rajput to surrender. Not possessing his ancestors' armies with which to cow the iron lady, Pratap nevertheless claimed victory by taking his own life and denying her the satisfaction of putting him in jail.

Today the Phool Bagh is a frayed-at-the-edges hotel with 15 acres of flowers and vegetable gardens. Mahendra Kumari runs it and is available to meet guests. Its lobby ranges from weird to wonderful. At the entrance Pratap's picture occupies a kind of altar. It is atop a carved wooden table, which rests on genuine elephant feet taken from expired family pets. Other items here include a ratty pink chaise longue, a picture of the Indian god Krishna, a map of Rajasthan, paintings of Alwar maharajas, photographs of horses, and a faded octagonal oriental rug. The dining room (you have to order your meals in advance) is dark and gloomy, though papered with floral wallpaper. Rooms are in Victorian era furniture that looks like castoffs from the royal attic. White tile baths are modern. The 13 rooms come in standard and deluxe. Deluxe are larger, but standards are also roomy. The hotel has no bar. The Phool Bagh also offers camping facilities.

Alwar 301 001, Rajasthan, India. Tel. 20253. AE, DC. Inexpensive.

Sariska Tiger Reserve and National Park

Although 22 tigers roam this 880 sq km of forest, rivers, and mountains some 35 km from Alwar, don't come here expecting to see one. They are sighted — but rarely. However, the blue bull antelope, sambar and spotted deer, wild boar, monitor lizards, and birds such as the spotted owl, golden-backed woodpecker, and grey partridge are enough to keep most nature lovers happy. Best time for animal watching is before the late June to September monsoons. You can book a jeep with driver who is knowledgeable about wildlife through the Sariska Palace Hotel.

Sariska Palace Hotel

Animal lovers have the hunter maharaja Jai Singh of Alwar to thank for both the Sariska Palace, located just outside the reserve's entrance, and the Sariska Tiger Reserve. The three-floor verandahed and cupolaed palace was the little something the maharaja built in 1900 to put up his royal buddies for a couple of days in the wilds. He came here every weekend bringing Indian princes and English viceroys for tiger shooting. The rigid etiquette of the court — along with 1,000 servants — accompanied him. Only princes and viceroys could stay on the first floor. The northern wing of the second floor was the maharaja's, the southern wing the maharani's. Each wing included both European and Indian kitchens. The building which is now the Bank of India housed Indian lords. Further south were a home for managers, a stable, and 40-car garage. All are intact today. North of the palace was the club house with swimming pool and band — available only to royals.

This extensive establishment was headed by a maharaja who was a practical joker. He once planted a stuffed tiger on the palace's verandah with a device hidden under the steps to make the tiger jump. Arm in arm with the British viceroy, the maharaja triggered the instrument as they neared the tiger. The viceroy quickly abandoned his British reserve.

But with Jai Singh's death, the palace came on hard times. It was virtually abandoned until it was bought in 1982 by the Sheeba Wheels Private Ltd. Corp. The firm undertook an extensive remodeling operation, peeling away imported wall paper that had been ruined and repairing fine old furniture. While knocking down walls, they discovered the palace's heating system, unfortunately only after it had been destroyed. Each room had a fireplace which heated a series of pipes, thus ensuring maximum use of the fire. Today, though, all 27 rooms are warmed by heaters.

The new owner's efforts have made the Sariska one of India's nicer small palace hotels. Rooms with 20-ft ceilings contain beautiful Victorian furniture. Spacious baths with original tiles (some with delicate floral patterns), marble sinks, and tubs are a delight. Best rooms are 105 and 111.

The management has ambitious plans for the old club house — now a ruin. They will convert it into a health club with swimming pool. But as you sit on the immaculate circular lawns listening to peacocks call and watching the varied bird life in front of the peach-hued palace, it seems as if the Sariska doesn't need another thing to make it complete.

Sariska, District Alwar, Rajasthan, India. Tel. 22, Sariska; 66804, Jaipur; 642413, 732365, 739712, New Delhi. AE, DC, MC, V. Expensive.

Bharatpur

The name of the game here in this eastern Rajasthan town is the Keoladeo Ghana National Park. Made up of marshes artificially created for the hunting pleasures of the maharaja of Bharatpur, the park is on the migration route of birds from China and Siberia. India's best bird sanctuary, Bharatpur draws birders from all over the world looking for that special bird for their life list. During the winter months many species of cranes, ducks, spoonbills, eagles, owls, shrikes, herons, and storks visit the sanctuary. Formerly the Siberian crane was common, but their numbers are decreasing. In 1990 only 10 were counted at the sanctuary.

Golbagh Palace Hotel

This is a hotel only for diehard palace fans. It is run-down, overpriced, and far from the bird sanctuary. Reports say new owners plan to renovate it, but in India time stretches into the next lifetime so don't hold your breath.

Rooms here open onto a central courtyard decorated with traditional ancestral pictures and Victorian-style clutter. The lounge has threadbare carpet and furnishings in need of a good polishing. The dining room comes with high-backed chairs and tiger heads over the fireplace. All of the 18 rooms are large and high-ceilinged, but unfortunately all are poorly maintained.

The Golbagh has potential, but until and unless it is given some care, the hotel is presently not worth a stay.

Bharatpur, Rajasthan, India. Tel. 3349. No Credit cards. Moderate.

Sawai Madhopur

Sawai Madhopur's claim to fame is that it is the village closest to Ranthambore National Park, India's world-famous tiger preserve.

It is estimated that 90% of all photos of Indian tigers are taken at Ranthambore. Because of the vision of one man, Fateh Singh Rathore, tigers here roam freely, unafraid of humans. As director of the park, Singh suspected that tigers were not naturally nocturnal, but hunted at night from fear of humans. But ridding the park of people was no easy feat. Villages had been there for over 200 years. While sympathizing with villagers reluctant to leave ancestral homes, Singh's first loyalty was to the tigers.

At one point he ended up in the hospital for six months, attacked by a peasant angry at being moved out of his home. But Singh eventually won his battle. Today the 392-square-km park is free of human habitation, and 40 tigers (from 14 at the park's inception) roam boldly throughout the day.

Along with tigers the park boasts 300 species of trees and over 100 species of grasses and seasonal plants.

Two hundred seventy-two species of birds have been sighted. But this is a park with many reminders of civilization as well. The fortress of **Ranthambore** sits in its center. Dating from the eleventh century, it is one of India's most ancient forts. It withstood assaults from generals and emperors from the thirteenth through sixteenth centuries. Later the maharaja of Jaipur owned it and used the surroundings as hunting grounds.

Castle Jhoomar Baori Forest Lodge

The Jhoomar looks more like a prince's castle than the hunting lodge that it was. Perched atop a hill surrounded by forest, the rust-red castle is full of hidden nooks, zanily-angled corners, and strangely-shaped rooms. Its whimsical architect evidently abhorred more conventional designs.

Twelve km from Ranthambore, it was formerly the hunting lodge of Jaipur Maharaja Madhor Singh, who at times lived here in the late nineteenth century. It has been run as a hotel by the Rajasthan Tourist Development Corp. since the 1960's.

With their odd angles, all standard rooms are individual. The small windows are framed with old wood. Decor is Rajasthani style with bright fabrics and woods. Baths and toilets are in their own tiny separate rooms. Upper floor rooms are your best bet since they have views of the forest and their own balconies. The three suites are a mass of arches and alcoves with exotic Rajasthani furnishings.

Each floor comes with its own small lounge done up with pillows and bolsters Indian-style.

The hotel has a bar and restaurant. In addition, it offers a variety of tours into the sanctuary.

Ranthambore Road, Sawai Madhopur 322 001, Rajasthan, India. Tel. 2495. No credit cards. 20% discount July-Sept. Inexpensive.

Jogi Mahal

This tiny lodge draws high marks for being the only inn inside the tiger sanctuary. Its location is superb — minutes away from the fort and right on a lake to which tigers often come to drink during the dry season. If you miss the tigers, you can content yourself with viewing deer and water fowl.

The Jogi's origins seem almost as ancient as the Ranthambore forest. The spot on which it rests, marked by India's second largest banyan tree (a shrine itself, mentioned in documents 500 years ago) has attracted spiritual seekers for centuries. The Jogi received its name from the yogis who once lived in the woods hundreds of years ago and slept on its grounds during their wanderings. Later it was said to be the residence of the temple priest. Fragmentary sculptures of Indian gods found in the Ranthambore forest rest on the hotel's grounds, reminding of the spiritual energy connected with this highly charged spot. More prosaically in later years it was used by the Jaipur maharaja's hunting parties as a lookout for spotting animals.

Today the rust-colored, six-room Jogi is run by the Rajasthan Forest Department. With simple rooms and no electricity, it is for adventurous travelers who don't mind roughing it in order to be close to the forest's mysterious pulse.

Rooms 1, 2, 5, and the dining hall are part of the old building. Rooms 3 and 4 were added in 1979. New rooms are larger with sitting areas and fireplaces. All baths are modern.

In recent years the hotel has become popular because of former prime minister Rajiv Gandhi's week-long stay.

Reservations are made through the field director's office.

Field Director, Ranthambore National Park, Sawai Madhopur. No credit cards. Closed July, August, September. Inexpensive (meals included with tariff).

Sawai Madhopur Lodge

Getting back to nature in the old days took a bit of doing. It meant packing hundreds of specially-made tents, furniture, and carpets, rounding up elephants and horses, and amassing an army of servants. Such were the efforts accompanying the maharajas' hunting forays from the property on which the Sawai Madhopur Lodge now sits. The garden became a Persian carpet of bright tents. Women, in *purdah,* had their own tents which sat in bullock carts, securely protecting their occupants from male eyes. The dirty work of the hunt was done by the many servants who accompanied the maharaja. They ran through the forest beating instruments. Gradually surrounding the tiger, who must have been driven senseless by the clamor, they lured him into the open for the royals to shoot.

The style of the hunt did not change with the building of the crescent-shaped, two-story hunting lodge in 1936 by Maharaja Man Singh. You can still see photos in its bar of people getting their jollies from killing tigers. Famous people, from the maharaja himself to Queen Elizabeth, stand proudly over their slain animals. However, the most striking photo, that of a half-crazed tiger charging an elephant, best captures both the danger and the pathos underlying a *shikara,* or hunt.

In recent years tiger hunting has been banned, but the Sawai Madhopur remained a hunting lodge until 1971 when it made the transition to a hotel. In 1987 the Taj Group assumed management.

Today the Sawai Madhopur retains much of the flavor of the old days when Man Singh came here with his beautiful third wife Gayatri Devi. Their rooms, now the Maharaja and Maharani Suites ($110), are upstairs, topping a winding staircase in the main building. Furniture in the suites is original; both contain delightfully eccentric writing desks old enough to be your grandmother's. Fixtures in baths are quaint relics. Standard rooms are in the small structures flanking the principal building. Formerly guest houses, they contain simple rooms with contemporary furnishings. Baths have showers only.

The hotel's most appealing parts are its public rooms. A wide verandah curving around the front of the building overlooks a generous lawn. Inside, both reception and lounge contain original murals depicting jungle scenes. In addition, there is a fireplace in the lounge which is popular during chilly winter evenings. The Sawai Madhopur also has a small swimming pool and a bar.

Located 20 minutes from Ranthambore, the hotel sits on 12 acres of old trees and gardens. It is rich in bird life. Here the chattering of the birds in the trees drowns out the distractions of the twentieth century and opens you to nature's heartbeat.

Ranthambore National Park Road, Sawai Madhopur 322 001, Rajasthan, India. Tel. 2541/2247, India; 1-800-ILUVTAJ, United States; 01-828-5909, United Kingdom. Telex c/o 3652254 RBAG IN, 3652147 RBAG IN. Fax c/o (0141)73798. AE, DC. Low season rates possible; contact U. S. Taj office. Expensive.

Kota

This city of 400,000 combines the medieval with the twentieth century. As Rajasthan's industrial heart, it is the home of various industries and an atomic power plant. But its spiritual heart belongs to times long before the enthronement of technology. Its river, the Chambal, was mentioned in the Upanishads. Kota's pace is leisurely and personal. Its women are often clad in saris featuring the distinctive weave brought from Mysore in the seventeenth century, and its men have colored turbans wound round their heads.

The centerpiece of Kota's sites is the eighteenth century **City Palace** located on the banks of the Chambal. Once a miniature city, the sprawling complex is now open to the public. Particularly outstanding is the **Rao Madho Singh Museum,** one of Rajasthan's best. It displays miniatures from the Kota school and murals. Also featured are Rajasthani weapons and dress.

Brijraj Bhawan Palace Hotel

Sitting on the grassy banks of the Chambal River, this white rambling structure has the leisurely feeling of the antebellum South. It makes you want to spend your days doing nothing but whiling away the hours on its wide semi-circular verandah watching life on the sleepy river flow along. You will be hovered over by beret-clad retainers who have been serving Kota's royal family for decades. Their technique is not as polished as that of luxury hotel employees, but their style, tempered by a bygone time when loyalty was as important as rupees, is warmer. This is a place where you can arrive late at night without a reservation, and although the hotel is full, they'll make room. It is a place where they'll run across town to make change for you, even though you might have to wait half the morning for someone to return. It is a place where life is still slowed to the pace of the human being.

Owned by Brijraj Singh, the 57-year-old son of Kota's ex-maharaja, it is run by an army of the family's employees. Singh, who manages family businesses, will see guests upon request, but generally has little to do with everyday operations. He lives in a separate wing of the Brijraj.

The Brijraj was built in the first half of the nineteenth century by the maharaja as a residence for British leaders. It saw fighting during the Indian mutiny in 1857. Later it became Kota's official state guest house. Queen Mary stayed here in 1911. After 1940 the maharaja lived in the building during the monsoons. In 1955 he deeded it to his son, who has made it his primary residence. In 1972 a portion of the Brijraj was made into a hotel.

Today it is Kota's top hotel with a clientele of businessmen. It is still largely undiscovered by tourists. But it is one of the best maintained of the family-run palace hotels and, with its riverside location and attentive staff, one of the most delightful.

The hotel has not been spruced up so much that it is postcard-perfect. Grass on the lawn in front of the verandah needs a cutting. It is tended by a turbaned man squatting on his haunches. Treasures from former days seem strewn about the grass at random, but here in this peaceful setting they are beautiful. A marble chair with *jalli* crisscrossing sits in the midst of overgrown grass. Various Hindu gods guard the lawn. Someone has placed a flower on one's head. Peacocks stroll, occasionally displaying their incandescent tails.

Inside the dining room are the stuffed heads of every animal unfortunate enough to have been shot by the maharaja. Guests sit together on high-backed wooden chairs around a long table. Dark wood cabinets flank walls holding raj-era silver. The hotel's seven rooms are all huge and high-ceilinged with old, well-preserved furniture. Baths are spacious.

Civil Lines, Kota 324 001, Rajasthan, India. Tel.23071.
No credit cards. Moderate.

Umaid Bhawan Palace Hotel

In the midst of peaceful, tree-filled grounds, the Umaid
Bhawan is the home of Kota's 83-year-old ex-maharaja.
A warren of a structure with countless arches and
courtyards, the Umaid was designed in 1905 by Sir
Swinton Jacob, who made a good living by creating
palaces for Indian princes.

In 1990 10 rooms of the structure were turned into a
hotel. It is run by the Brijraj Palace Hotel people.

Rooms and baths here bear the lavishness of space and
high ceilings of older buildings. Entered from wide
marble halls, they feature interesting old furnishings
from the Brijraj Hotel. For those who don't mind sleeping with the energy from killed animals, room 16 features a stuffed tiger. Many rooms open onto
black-and-white marble terraces. All bathtubs are
charmingly antique. Lounge and dining room are filled
with massive raj-era wooden furniture and the standard heads of slaughtered game.

Of the two hotels, the Brijraj is the better choice. It is
lighter and brighter in feeling and located on the river.
But the Umaid Bhawan, too, makes you feel as if you
are living in another historical time.

Brijraj Hotel, Civil Lines, Kota 324 001, Rajasthan,
India. Tel. 23071. No credit cards or bar (beer only).
Moderate.

Mandawa

The childless Hindu king asked help of the Muslim saint, who told him that his wife would bear him a male heir. But the baby had to be washed in the blood of a cow. Indeed, in nine months a boy was born to the couple. But being a Hindu and believing that cows were sacred, the king could not stand to kill a cow. Instead, he settled on a goat and bathed his child in the blood of that animal.

Later, meeting the saint, he confessed that he had not exactly followed the holy man's orders. The Muslim nodded, as if he already knew. "Your boy will grow up to be a king," he predicted, "but because you did not bathe him with the blood of the cow, a great and strong animal, his kingdom will not be great and strong. It will be a lesser one, as is the goat, a small and weak animal."

Thus the king's son, Rao Shekha, founder of the Shek-havati region north of Jaipur, came to rule. His was to be a prosperous region, fueled by trade to China along ancient caravan routes, but not one of the major Rajas-thani states. Generations later Nawal Singh, ruler of a Shekhavati city (Jhunjhunu), deeded his two sons Man-dawa, another Shekhavati city, and his Mandawa castle. In 1790 the brothers moved to the castle, built in 1755, the first of nine generations of their family to live there.

Today the castle is still the centerpiece of a town of 20,000 composed of 60% Hindus and 40% Muslims. Some 168 km from Jaipur, Mandawa also boasts 200 homes of art. These houses painted inside and out with a wide range of geometric and floral frescoes, in addition to scenes depicting Indian gods, everyday life, and even the Wright brothers and their airplane, are owned by rich merchants who earned their fortunes in Mandawa and later moved to larger cities. All the top business names in India except for the Bombay Tatas began in Shekhavati. Although no longer in their home towns except on special occasions, these business barons are in a sense still present in the works of art they bequeathed to their city.

Castle Mandawa

The gong is still struck every hour, marking the passage of time as it has since the castle's birth in 1755. A massive door with spikes, protecting against dangers once imminent but now forgotten, guards the inner courtyard. Blackened with age, four towers stand guard at the castle's corners, gunholes intact. Frescoes, the earliest one painted in 1790, still adorn walls, alcoves, and hidden corners. The Castle Mandawa puts you in touch with the past. With a cobblestone courtyard, a red and yellow flag sporting the family crest, and aging walls stained by time, the 100-plus-room structure looks every inch a castle. At night vaulted by a full, uncluttered sky, framed by romantic castle cupolas, you feel as if you are master of your world on this powerful spot, as perhaps did the seven generations of nobles who lived here before it became a hotel. Luckily the transition to hotel has not killed the castle's spirit. You sense the passage of time here, but also the warmth of the present through members of the Singh family who run

Painted houses, Mandawa

Castle Mandawa Hotel, Mandawa

Rambagh Palace Hotel, Jaipur   *Jahangir Mahal, Orchha (right)*

it. They are the eighth generation from the one that first occupied Mandawa in 1790. Their 92-year-old grandfather lives in another part of the building.

Ever the gracious hosts, the handsome brothers are often in the verandah-style lobby answering questions and explaining family history. They dine with guests at dinners, which in winter are held around a fire with seating at *chokis,* low wooden tables often carved and decorated with brass. In summer months, sitting on the ground leaning back on bolsters, guests dine in the garden. Nearby is a family cannon that was used to defend the castle (minor skirmishes, no major battles). Sixty-flve-year-old Mathrin, with magnificent moustaches fairly bristling, whose family has been with the Singhs for three generations, dances Rajasthani-style, fueled by the two pegs of whiskey with which the family rewards him before each dance.

But it is perhaps at festival time when past and present most jubilantly fuse. Holidays in this small town are not something cooked up by the hotel, but are part of the long relationship between the Singh family and Mandawans. Although the Singhs no longer rule the land, they nonetheless are respected by the villagers, who do not easily break traditional ties. During the Gangaur festival in March-April the statues of the Indian gods Shiva and Parvati, which are kept at the castle, are dressed by a woman family member and carried to the Krishna temple on the palace grounds. There they are marched around the well of the castle at sunset so that water, a holy substance in Hinduism, may witness their wedding. After the wedding of the two gods is performed, they are taken back to the courtyard where the village women dance in celebration.

Sheesh Mahal Palace Hotel, Orchha

At the Holi festival, also in the spring, the villagers start dancing the night before. The next morning they dust colored powders on each other and then on the Singh family. Afterwards they dance again. The Singhs give each man a rupee for a drink, but the men wait until they are back at the village before they start boozing. They do not drink in front of the family as a sign of respect.

Finally, at Dussehra in October the Singhs call neighboring Rajputs, who appear dressed in swords and turbans, for lunch.

The establishment's 40 hotel rooms also contribute to the castle's medieval ambience. Tucked away in an exotic labyrinth of passages and staircases, no two are alike. With modifications and additional building, each generation of Singhs has added its stamp to the castle. Accordingly, each room bears the aura of the time in which it was created. Royal Suite 302 ($55) is on two levels with marble stairs connecting bedroom and sitting room. Entering by a 200-year-old carved wood door, you find seating which is Indian-style — pillows and bolsters — and a beautiful *choki* table under an arcade of arches. Royal Suite 308 ($55) was part of the *zenana,* the women's quarters. You can see the filigreed windows through which they gazed at the outside. Old pictures belonged to the Singh brothers' grandmother, who was in *purdah* throughout her life.

Approximately $5 more than standard doubles, deluxe doubles 208-210 ($25), also part of the *zenana,* contain frescoes, arches, and old doors. *Jarokhas,* the lattice windows through which cloistered women viewed the world, are still present. Standard doubles and singles have beds on marble platforms with curtains and bedspreads of fabric tie-dyed in the Mandawa style.

The owners also operate a nearby Desert Village set amid the sand dunes, where guests can ride camels. There is also a swimming pool. Rooms here are tribal-style mud huts, but with all modern amenities.

Hotel Castle Mandawa, Mandawa, Dist. Jhunjhunu Shekhavati, Rajasthan 333 704, India, tel. 24. Reservations: Mandawa House, Sansar Chandra Road, Jaipur 302 001. Tel. 75358. Telex 365 2342 CMDW IN. AE, DC, MC, V. Moderate.

Udaipur

Rajasthan's desert loses its harshness in Udaipur. This city, with its lakes and hills, honors beauty. Artists work in tiny studios designing *pichwais,* paintings on cloth, with paints from crushed stones. Even crumbling buildings are often graced with the native wall art.

But this lovely city has a backbone of steel. Alone of all the Rajasthan cities, Udaipur never recognized the British as governors of India. An Udaipur maharana (the Udaipur term for maharaja) was famous for snubbing the British by not turning up at their festivities. His final insult was not supporting the Brits in World War I.

Udaipur's centerpiece is the **City Palace.** Located on the eastern shores of Lake Pichola, the 1500-ft-long palace was begun by the city's founder Udai Singh in the sixteenth century and added to by succeeding maharanas. Part of the palace is now a museum. Particularly outstanding are the museum's displays of colored glass and mirrorwork.

North of the City Palace on Pichola's shores is **Jagdish Temple.** Dedicated to Jagdish, an aspect of the god Vishnu, the complex has a black stone image of this deity. Also impressive are the many carvings. The temple was built in 1651.

Much of Udaipur's life centers around its man-made **Lake Pichola.** The lake calls for a sunset boat trip (available at the Lake Palace Hotel). The boat stops at **Jag Mandir,** one of Udaipur's two water palaces. Unlike the Lake Palace, this one is uninhabited. Set on an island, the palace is one of Rajasthan's most beautiful. It is now barren, occupied by only a few pigeons, but its yellowed marble, domes, and inlaid stones in delicate designs hint of past splendors. It was built for Prince Khurram, who later became Shah Jahan, creator of the Taj Mahal. He stayed here in 1623-5 while battling his father for the Mughal throne. It was here he drew inspiration from the inlaid stone work that he would incorporate into the Taj.

Back on land the **Bharatiya Lok Kala Mandal Museum** is also worth a visit. Dedicated to displaying folk crafts, it has toys, dresses, masks, musical instruments, and especially puppets.

Lake Palace Hotel

The Lake Palace is probably India's most beautiful hotel. Other hotels might have grander architecture and flashier materials, but in some strange way that could perhaps occur only in India the Lake Palace Hotel moves the spirit. It seems alive, shimmering like the waters in which it rests. Sometimes the building is white, sometimes golden, sometimes pink. Never the same, at times it is like a floating mirage; at other times it seems earthbound, resting solidly in its lake as it has for almost 250 years.

From its inception this was a special palace, designed to make the beauty of each hour come alive. Different parts capture sun and moonlight, winds, and water, highlighting the movement of the day. It was built by Maharana Jagat Singh II on a small island near the northern shores of Lake Pichola. He named it Jag Niwas, after himself. At the water palace's inauguration on February 1, 1746, 29 ladies from the court, in addition to an army of mistresses and maids, were at the ceremony. The maharana gifted his noblemen with pedigreed horses and his bards with elephants and jewelry. The party lasted for three days.

In subsequent years the palace was used to entertain guests. One visitor describes the flurry of activity when arriving at the palace. Servants quickly furnished it with carpets and awnings. Cooks prepared meals. Champagne flowed. *Nautch* (dancing) girls performed. In the years before the Lake Palace was turned into a hotel in 1963, the maharanas used it as a summer palace. Arjun Singh, the brother of the last maharana, remembers riding the boat across the lake and sitting with the maharana and "so many courtiers."

The royal family ran the Lake Palace during its first years as a hotel. Vivien Leigh stayed here in its initial period, as did Britisher John Profumo, who retreated to the Lake Palace shortly after the scandal of his affair with call girl Christine Keeler. In 1971 the Lake Palace was turned over to the Taj group to manage. The union between hotel chain and royal family has been a happy one. The Taj's general manager Deepak Dutt, even though not from Rajasthan, has become a knowledge-able and enthusiastic advocate of the region and a repository of Lake Palace history. The brother of the current maharana sits on the board of directors and is a frequent visitor here.

But more than any other palace hotel, the Lake Palace doesn't need a maharaja to create a royal ambience. This white marble 85-room structure is the very image of what a fairy-tale palace should look like. From the moment you step into the motor launch that will trans-port you to the Lake Palace, you feel you are in a magical place. Inside, the lounge is done Indian-style: bolsters, Indian fabrics, and furniture with stout, low legs. There is much of the native colored glass work as well. Off the lounge the lily pond takes up an entire courtyard. It is presided over by a tiny statue of an Indian god that belonged to the maharana. Overlooking the water is an Udaipur mural, a glittering procession of women.

Both the restaurant and coffee shop face the pond. The coffee shop is in the part of the hotel designed by its architects for sitting and soaking up views. Facing the lake as well as the lily pond, this is where maharanas whiled away afternoons.

In the back of the hotel is the swimming pool. Although small, it was left as is because it is the pool of the maharanas. The Lake Palace also has a sauna and small gym. Upstairs there is a terrace with the maharanas' sundial. Nearby is a small starkly white cupola with chairs underneath for sitting and watching the lake. A favorite spot for photographers, the cupola appeared in PBS's *Jewel in the Crown*.

Suites here range from beautiful to historically authentic. The hands-down winner of the beauty contest is the Khush Mahal ($450). Here a large teak swing is suspended by golden chains from the ceiling. Furniture in crisscross *jalli* surrounds an oriental carpet in the sitting room. But the outstanding feature is the small enclosed balcony with colored glass windows. Their light makes the suite sparkle or brood, depending upon the mood of the day.

Other suites are less romantic, but include authentic touches. The Kamal Mahal's ($325) outstanding features are the colored glass inlay and ivory miniatures in the dining and dressing rooms. Both are from palace days. The suite also includes European wooden tables and desk. Also with some original furniture, including a chandelier of Belgium glass, is Sarvaritu ($450). Bedecked by mirrors and lithographs of the British army, this suite has an alcove with the Udaipur inlaid glass.

The most intriguing historically is the Maharana Suite ($450) which has 230-year-old paintings so detailed you need a magnifying glass to fully appreciate them. Its walls are equally old. They are in plaster made from ground mollusk shells, milk, and honey. Furniture is intricate, carved walnut made by local artisans. Also noteworthy is a 150-year-old onyx lamp designed to resemble flowers and leaves. An entire wall of the bedroom is painted with a mural. Above the bed is a mirror designed to catch precisely the fourteenth day of moonlight and reflect it on the bed. The marble balcony from which the maharana gave his audiences is still intact. Also interesting is a special conference room. Before the ceiling was repainted in 1939, it was covered with erotic paintings. Maharana Bhopal Singh would come here and enjoy what was probably India's most fascinating ceiling. Still in good condition are the two-century-old gilt frames and Belgium mirrors. Standard rooms have modern furnishings with Indian touches. Most overlook the brooding City Palace across the lake. An alternative are numbers 253 and 254, which are on the other side of the hotel and are not favored by guests because of their lack of City Palace views. However, these rooms offer fine sunset views and contain original tiles and glasswork. This fanciful hotel has a final romantic touch. You can rent the 95-year-old launch, the *Gangaur*. Formerly this was a festival boat reserved for the maharana's use. But in these more democratic times anyone can book the *Gangaur* for parties or dinners.

Pichola Lake, Udaipur 313 001, Rajasthan, India. Tel. (0294)23241-5; 1-800-ILUVTAJ, United States; (01)828-5909, United Kingdom. Telex 33 203 LPAL IN. AE, DC, MC, V. Very expensive.

Laxmi Vilas Palace Hotel

On a hill overlooking Fateh Sagar lake in northern Udaipur, this two-story palace with an abundance of cupolas lost much of its royal ambience when it became a part of the government's ITDC chain. You won't find family members or employees that have grown up with the building here. Staff knows little about the building's history. Everything seems imported, down to the furniture, which comes from Delhi.

Still, with its wings and many cupolas, the hotel presents a fanciful exterior. The lake seems magical here. Peaceful and far above the city's clutter, the hotel's hilltop site also creates an aura.

This hotel does not have the high gloss of the Lake Palace or Shivniwas, but the prices are somewhat lower. Its standard services make it a suitable choice for the budget-minded who want something different but don't want to dispense with international hotel standards. Some of the rooms here could stand sprucing up. Decor in standard rooms is simple with dark wood setting the theme. All rooms in the new wing have either city or lake views, although the hotel's driveway in front cuts down on their impact.

Standard doubles are approximately two-thirds of the size of the four doubles (numbers 120-22 and 221) in the old wing. There rooms are larger and have the high ceilings of an older building. The flagship suite is the Maharani ($100), a roomy affair with oriental carpet, overstuffed velvet chairs, etched glass doors, and tiger head over the fireplace. This suite comes with a balcony and city views. In addition, the hotel offers six royal suites ($82) with less spectacular furnishings.

Before its present incarnation as a hotel the Laxmi Vilas was a royal guest house for lower level diplomats. Built in 1929 by Maharana Bhopal Singh, it became an ITDC hotel in 1969. In 1973 part of the new wing was built; the other part was completed in 1988.

Udaipur 313 001, Rajasthan, India. Tel. (0294) 24411-3. Telex 033-218. Low season rates possible with negotiation. AE, MC, V. Expensive.

Rangniwas Hotel

A sign at the registration desk of the 22-room Rangniwas Hotel reads: "Do not hesitate to bombard us with questions. It will be a pleasure to satisfy you with most authentic information."

The tone at this well-run budget hotel down the road from the Shivniwas is informal. The prices are low. The history is full.

Built 150 years ago by Maharana Fateh as a guest house for one of the princes, the building got its name from the prince's habit of dying his long beard to match his outfits. *Rang* means colorful; *niwas* is residence. In 1959 the property was given to Arjun Singh, natural brother of one of the maharanas. (Singh's brother was adopted by the maharana in order to have an heir.)

"With the change of times," says Singh, "I found the house very big." In 1969 he turned it into a hotel, one of the first homes run by the owner and his family to be converted to a hotel.

Part of its charm is that the rooms in the main building look as if they have scarcely changed since then.

With the most expensive rooms (numbers 1,2,5, and 6) going for approximately $10, furnishing is minimal and there is little attempt to create ambience. Still, some of the rooms have old, though poorly maintained, furniture, discards from royal days. Each of these ample doubles has a dressing room and large bath. However, rooms 1 and 6 have Indian-style (holes in the floor) toilets only.

At slightly lower prices are rooms 3 and 4. These rooms are smaller, with Indian-style toilets. Baths include shower only. A plus here are balconies. Rooms 1-5 are air-cooled. All rooms have ceiling fans.

Opposite the main house in what was the servants' quarters are the 12 rooms completed in 1990. Smaller than those in the old building, these are spiffier than their elderly cousins. All have Western-style toilets. The old house and servants' quarters enclose a large garden in which guests may lounge. Separate is the restaurant, run by Mrs. Singh. There is no bar, but the hotel sells beer.

The Singh family takes an active role in running the Rangniwas. They seem genuinely to care about guests. True to the lobby sign, they are sources of excellent practical information, such as where to get the cheapest auto rickshaw and how to tour Udaipur.

Having seen the royal era fall to the democratic one, Arjun can regale you with tales of the old days. He, for instance, remembers his family's being awakened at 3 AM by the maharana's courtiers. They were there to take his older brother to the palace because the maharana had chosen him as his heir. What Singh most remembers was not the honor of having his brother chosen to become maharana, but the sadness of losing his sibling.

Lake Palace Road, tel. (0294) 23891. No low season rates. No credit cards. Inexpensive.

Shikarbadi Hotel

In Maharana Bhagwat Singh's days a trip to Shikarbadi, his hunting lodge, was a time of roughing it. Although only 5 km from Udaipur, the area was covered with dense forest. Singh hunted the large numbers of panthers and lions on elephant back. A generation later his younger son Arvind Singh — although also a hunter — prefers to protect the animals rather than kill them. They attract visitors intent on appreciating wildlife instead of destroying it.

Although the forest and tigers have disappeared, there is still a feeling of being in the country in spite of Shikarbadi's proximity to Udaipur. Set in the fields and hills on 500 acres, it seems far from people and close to nature. With beamed ceilings, rough stone walls, jute matting on the floors, and wicker furniture, its 25 rooms carry out the rustic theme.

The hotel comprises the main building, made in 1935, and the new block, created in 1977 when Arvind turned Shikarbadi into a hotel. Rooms in the old block are larger, with sitting rooms. They also contain antique furniture. However, the smaller new rooms work better here. They are cozy, with decor suitable for a nature lodge.

The two-story old building contains a small library, bar, and restaurant. In the main lounge notice the chandelier of the requisite Belgium crystal and the ivory miniatures.

Outside there is a deer park containing spotted deer running free within an enclosure. With the restaurant facing the park, you can eat your meals watching the animals. The property also has an artificial lake, which is full half the year, plenty of monkeys, and a stud farm. Raising horses is one of Arvind's passions. He often comes to Shikarbadi to ride or look over his animals.

Guests can rent horses for riding. The hotel also offers horse safaris to surrounding areas.

Although the presence of a park with captive animals reduces Shikarbadi's charms, its peace and natural beauty, nonetheless, will appeal to nature lovers.

Photography buffs shouldn't miss Vardhba, the 85-year-old gatekeeper. Vardhba's face carries the wisdom of India and the saltiness of the Rajasthani peasant.

Goverdhanvilas, Udaipur 313 001, Rajasthan, India. Tel. (0294)83200-4. Telex 0335-227BADI IN. Fax 0294-23823 (Central Office). Fifty per cent discount April 1 to September 30. AE, DC, MC, V. Moderate.

Shivniwas

A guard stands at the gate warding off untoward characters. Even in these democratic times, the Shivniwas is definitely the land of royalty. With impeccable lineage linked to the City Palace, this hotel boasts memorabilia from the palace and the royal family, who lives in it. Guests at the Shivniwas can request appointments with owner Arvind Singh, the maharana's younger brother. Ordinarily, though, the family keeps to themselves, guarded by loyal retainers. But you feel their presence here. Right down to key chains of the sun, the family's insignia, on the doorkeys, the Shivniwas is an abode of kings. The royals used to bring their visitors here to the 100-year-old former royal guest house. The Shah of Iran, Jacqueline Onassis, and the Nepalese king have all stayed at the Shivniwas. Roger Moore occupied a royal suite, the Red Room, while filming the James Bond movie *Octopussy*.

Furnishings come from the City Palace. When the housekeeping staff decides a piece has had its day, they cart it back to the City Palace and exchange it for another. Much of the furniture is delicately carved fine old wood in the European style that seemed to appeal to the maharajas. Most rooms have century-old paintings as well, depicting both royal and city life.

The Shivniwas' 14 standard rooms are separate from the main courtyard, distancing them from the elegance that permeates the rest of the hotel. Although sofas and chairs in standards are modern, all rooms have pieces from the palace. Standard rooms contain only showers and are fan-cooled, rather than air conditioned. Rooms 21 and 22 are two of the better ones.

But the Shivniwas comes into its own with its suites. They are exquisitely turned out in both turn-of-the-century and new furnishings designed to keep the suite's theme. Each of the eight individually furnished deluxe suites ($100) has a terrace and balcony with view. Suites 14-16 have lake views, 11 has city/lake, 12 lake/garden, and 8-10 city views. All bathrooms in these suites have stunning vistas of the lake.

The five historical suites ($140) also have their own views with private balconies, but here the quality of furniture is higher and includes such period pieces as a four-poster bed trimmed in steel (probably once the latest European fad), a carved wood desk with leather top, and an antique desk set with lamp. Such suites are spacious, consisting of sitting room, bedroom, luggage room, dressing room, and bath — all with views. Baths are in marble.

But the Shivniwas' Cinderella suites are her royal ones, the Red Suite and the Blue Suite ($225). Here walls inlaid in the Udaipur fashion with century-old colored glass vie with ivory-inlaid wooden doors, and carefully chosen modern and antique furniture such as French carpets and a marvelous old *choki,* the short-legged table designed for floor seating, with ivory inlay.

The hotel also has a small marble swimming pool.

No visit to the Shivniwas would be complete without a drink at her bar. A former ceremonial hall, it is decked out from floor to ceiling with Udaipur's beautiful colored glass. In addition, it sports a chandelier of Belgium crystal, antique mirrors, easy chairs, and garden views. On either side of the ivory-inlaid wooden entrance doors are glass murals of elephants — one side depicting the African elephant, the other the Indian. A few years ago this room was stuffed with crystal furniture--even down to a crystal bed. Eventually the royal family tired of this rather bizarre display and carted the lot off to the palace, passing on to the attendants there the problem of just what one does with a crystal bed.

Shivniwas Palace, Udaipur, 313 001, Rajasthan, India. Tel. 28239-41. Telex 033-226 IPAL IN. Cable PALACE. Fax, 029423823. AE, DC, MC, V. Moderate.

THIS ROYAL HAS DEMOCRATIC LEANINGS

Arvid Singh, younger brotherof the Udaipur maharana, sits in his Shivniwas apartment. The room is full of ornate French furniture, photos of family members with dignitaries, and an exercycle. *Noddy and the Toddles*, a children's books, rests on a nearby table. In a plain white Nehru suit, the bearded Singh has decided to go to the temple. Appointments will not stand in his way.

"Talk to my wife," he says in a voice that invites no argument. "It will be good to get a woman's point of view."

A servant calls Vijay Raj Kumari, 45, a brown-haired woman in a plain sari. She flashes her husband a look of annoyance for dumping his obligations on her, but it has gone after a microsecond. She quickly smiles and offers tea. With a gentle presence, she is gracious throughout the interview.

From the royal family in Kutch, an area in the western state of Gujarat, the convent-educated Vijay grew up in a sheltered life. Her mother was in *purdah*. Her marriage to Arvind was an arranged one, auspiciously uniting the two royal families.

Because of a complicated lawsuit between Arvind and the maharana, Vijay's role soon became greater than just that of wife of the maharaja's younger brother. Many have taken Arvind's side in this family feud and regard him as the maharana and Vijay the maharani.

In carrying out her functions, Vijay is busy from 7:00 to 9:00 with appointments, the telephone, and her three children. From 9:00 to 10:30 she tends to her office and finishes with phone calls. Afternoons are reserved for her children, who return from school at 2:45. She is active in their school. Evenings are reserved for official functions. "There's always something going on," she laments. "It takes so much out of you."

The family is popular with Udaipurians. "People," she says, "are very kind, very affectionate. So many things you have to stick to because of them."

It is only away from Udaipur that Vijay feels she can be herself. "You want to do so many things, but you don't want to hurt feelings." Bombay's a particular delight because "nobody's watching you."

You feel that this woman would exchange all the titles in a second for a normal life. She chose a public school for her children. Started by her father-in-law for bright but poor kids, it was the best one in Udaipur, according to Vijay. She celebrates that going to school with "the driver's son, the maid's son" her children will "learn a certain street smarts."

She wants them to be "hard-working, to have a trade because a trade gives them freedom. There's no shame in getting a job."

Vijay says she hopes to provide a positive role model by being a good worker herself. She pauses, as if recalling the lavish times when her family ruled Kutch. "Thank God everything changed gradually," she muses. But this is a woman who seems to be attracted to the freedom of democratic times. "It's much better to be working," she declares emphatically. You suspect if she could choose her next life, it would be an ordinary one, just like everyone else.

Mt. Abu

Mt. Abu is Rajasthan without its desert, with trees and flowers instead of the dry land. Located on a 1200-meter-high plateau, Mt. Abu is Rajasthan's only hill station, cool even during India's hottest months. Peak times here are May, June, October, and November. It is necessary to reserve rooms in advance during these months.

Mt. Abu's greatest attractions are the **Dilwara Temples** 5 kms out of town. At these Jain temples white marble is carved so that it appears as delicate as spun sugar. Filling pillars and ceilings with a forest of forms, artists here eschewed empty spaces. The temples are not to be missed, some of the finest in a region which has pushed stone carving to unequalled heights.

In the center of town is **Nakki Lake**, encircled by its wall of green hills.It also has a number of distinctive rock carvings. A fourteenth-century temple stands on its shores.

Bikaner Palace

Amid 20 acres of gardens and lawns in Mt. Abu's hills, this red sandstone building was once owned by the maharaja of Bikaner. He used to nip off to Mt. Abu when Bikaner's summer heat became too much. It was designed by an Indian architect and built in 1885. A new wing was added in 1988. Today it is still in the Bikaner family, owned by Madhulika Kumari, daughter of the last maharaja. She visits during summers. The 38-room hotel is managed by royal family members.

Here the raj-era furniture and lush gardens can't charm you out of noting the building's poor maintenance. Walls are stained and furniture tatty. The building could use a good cleaning and painting. Advantages include ample high-ceilinged rooms and baths. However, they seem to bear a century's worth of dust.

A bizarre feature is the gallery of photos of downed animals lining the staircase walls. They, along with the mandatory stuffed animals in the lounge, attest to the family's love of the *shikara,* the royal hunt.

You would not want to go out of your way to stay at the Bikaner. Although prices are moderate, many other palace hotels have similar tariffs with better maintenance and service.

Delwara Road, Mount Abu 307 501. Tel. 21, 33. Telex 0365 2700 ABUIN 008. AE, DC, MC, V. Moderate.

Connaught House

This cozy hotel has impeccable royal credentials. Owned by the maharaja of Jodhpur and formerly the official summer residence of Sir Donald Field, chief minister of Jodhpur, it consists of the original six-room cottage and a new wing of nine rooms built in 1986. Nestled in a pleasantly overrun garden perpetually full of birdsong, this inn is close to the city center and is within walking distance of Nakki Lake.

Rooms in the cottage are large, but dark. They are simply furnished with turn-of-the-century hand-me-downs. Stay here if you prefer the ambience of the ages in your room. New wing rooms open onto a verandah with good city views. These rooms are brighter but smaller than those in the cottage. Furniture and beds on green marble platforms give a clean and uncluttered feeling. The new rooms could be in any moderately-priced Indian hotel. The tiny lounge and dining room are a jumble of memorabilia, from a bust of Victoria to an 1848 painting of a horseshoeing.

Although not of palatial proportions, the Connaught House is a cleaner and more charming choice than Mt. Abu's other palace hotel, the Bikaner. Its major drawback is that it does not serve meals during the low summer season.

c/o Umaid Bhawan Palace, Jodhpur, 342 006 Rajasthan, India. Tel. 22316, Umaid Bhawan; 260 Mt. Abu. Telex 0552-202 UPB IN. No credit cards. Moderate.

Jodhpur

Jodhpur is a long way from everything, making this 500-year-old city bordering on Rajasthan's Thar desert romantic and remote.

One of the most enjoyable experiences you will probably have here is talking to Jodhpur's turbaned men and veiled women. You get a sense of the slow pace of their lives, more in tune to the rhythms of the desert than the rush of the twentieth century. They are less likely to inflate prices and more inclined to regard you as a human being — if a somewhat strange species — rather than a walking dollar sign.

The city's main historical attraction is **Meherangarh Fort.** This massive, battle-scarred structure with commanding views of the city has a museum containing items belonging to the long line of Jodhpur kings, hand-prints of rulers' wives who voluntarily killed themselves upon the deaths of their husbands, eighteenth-century cannons, and royal suites.

Also interesting is the old capital **Mandore,** 9 km from Jodhpur, with gardens containing cenotaphs of Jodhpur maharajas. The other site worth a visit is the **Umaid Bhawan Palace,** which now serves as hotel, residence of the maharaja, and small museum. The museum contains clocks and other European-style memorabilia maharajas were fond of collecting. But more interesting are its guides, the maharaja's oldest servants. Bastiram, 82, has been with the royal family since 1922 and delights in reminiscing.

Umaid Bhawan Palace Hotel

Perhaps the real beginning of the Umaid predates its actual building. It commences with a holy man's curse. He pronounced that a good reign in the Rathore dynasty would be followed by years of drought. Thus in the 1920's, after the 50-year rule of Pratap Singh, this desert city was beseiged with drought and famine. Those who tell the story point out that the tough peasants did not ask for a handout, but rather pleaded with Maharaja Umaid Singh to give them work. In response, Singh did what any pleasure-loving monarch would do. He commissioned British architect H. V. Lanchester to design a palace. Lanchester had worked closely with Sir Edwin Lutyens, designer of New Delhi's government buildings. As a result, the Umaid with its dome and columns is reminiscent of the New Delhi government center.

As befitting a project whose purpose was to create employment, construction of the palace was leisurely. The foundation stone was laid in 1929, but the royal family did not move until 1943. The maharaja employed 2,000 to 3,000 people during the building years. Many have criticized Singh for the extravagance of making a palace so close to Indian independence, but they forget that, without it, countless Jodhpur citizens would not have survived the famine.

The Umaid's construction was carried out with that special Indian approach to the practical. Planners chose the hill on which the palace rests, but did not foresee that the site was without a nearby water supply and was solid rock, making it difficult for anything to grow. In addition, it was far from the quarry site supplying the sandstone with which it was built.

But no matter. You can make miracles when you're a maharaja. The royals found donkeys to lug soil to the hill, dug through the rock for water, and made a railroad to transport the stone. Once on the hill, the sandstone was hewn into large blocks with interlocking joints. In the end they would fit together without mortar and be a monument in stone to the Rajasthani people's perseverance.

The result of their labors was a dun-colored sandstone palace flanked by two wings. The structure contained 347 rooms, many courtyards, and a banquet hall seating 300. Even today it is regarded as an outstanding example of the Beaux Arts style. But sadly the elegant palace would not come into its own for many years. Forty-three-year-old Maharaja Umaid Singh had lived in it only four years when he died in 1947. His successor

Hanwit Singh also died young. Ironically Hanwit had just won a landslide victory in the 1952 elections and was on his way home to celebrate when his plane crashed. His son Gaj Singh II converted the Umaid into a hotel in 1971.

Today, in keeping with the tone set by Gaj, a maharaja who prefers study tour groups to the general ones, the Umaid's atmosphere is refined. Guests might encounter the maharaja, who swims in the pool and uses the front entrance like everyone else. That entrance is decorated with the Rathore coat of arms and leads to a lobby of polished black granite followed by lounge areas in pink sandstone and marble. The hotel's centerpiece is its 103-ft inner dome capped by an outer one 43 ft higher.

Furnishings in public rooms are either from the fort or were made by Jodhpur craftspeople. Most are gilt and look as if they came from Louis XIV's court. Carpets in the Risala dining room were woven epecially for the palace by Kashmiri rugmakers. The cavernous restaurant was formerly the banquet hall. When compared to similar Rajastani luxury hotels, prices for meals are steep. The restaurant serves both buffet lunch and dinner.

The Umaid also has an indoor swimming pool decorated with signs of the zodiac, a health club, and a library. Trimmed in trophies and tusks, its bar features an odd stuffed bear holding a drink at the entrance.

A favorite spot is the terrace overlooking the expansive lawn and gardens. Even though the hotel charges a king's ransom to non-guests for drinks here, it is a fine place to down a cold one while watching the palace peacocks and a Jodhpur sunset. The white marble pavilion on the grass was brought from one of the family's old gardens.

The hotel's two Royal Suites ($555), appropriately named the Maharaja and Maharani since the royal couple lived in them, maintain their original art deco style. Rooms are spacious, baths roomy and luxurious. The Maharani features parquet floors, a terrace with garden views, a small kitchen, and a black and peach bedroom. Over the bed is a mural of a woman perched on a lion. The bathtub is carved out of a single piece of pink marble. The Maharaja Suite is more masculine with leopard skin furniture, black marble floors, a curving mirrored dome over the bed, and murals of horsemen. Murals in both suites were done by a WW II Polish refugee.

The four Regal Suites ($390) have large sitting, dressing, and bedrooms with fort views and fireplaces. The nine Luxury Suites ($170) are smaller. All feature period furniture. Perks for suite guests include a champagne breakfast and limo service to and from the airport. If limos are too twentieth century for your taste, you can choose a horse and carriage instead.

Standard rooms are sizable with modern furnishings.

The Umaid also celebrates the following Indian festivals:

Holi in March-April when Indians dump colored water on each other. The maharaja describes the hotel's Holi as a "free-for-all on the lawn."

Singh's birthday falling between December 15 and January 15. All clansmen and extended family in full regalia come to greet their maharaja.

Horse Festival in October. Singh invites people to show off their best horses.

Full moon in October when the entire building is lit up and musicians perform on the lawn.

The hotel sponsors train trips to the desert city of Jaisalmer in the cars owned by the maharaja's grand-father. The Umaid emphasizes that by today's stand-ards they are not luxurious; they do not, for instance, have air conditioning. But they come with loads of character and allow passengers to experience travel the royal way.

Jodhpur 342 006, Rajasthan, India. Tel. 22316, 22516, 22366, India; 1-800-223-0888, United States and Canada; 441-541-1199, London; 0-800-282-811, rest of United Kingdom. Telex 0552-202 UBP IN. AE, DC, MC, V. Low rates possible for long term stays. Very expensive.

OF FLOWER CHILDREN AND KINGS

You feel you are chatting with the guy next door. Except he isn't. This handsome 42-year-old with eyes soulful enough to soften the hardest heart is the maharaja of Jodhpur.

"I would have been the maharaja," Gaj Singh corrects, "but I don't have a state any more. I am as any other citizen."

Sort of. No matter that he lives in a palace, possibly the world's largest home, and that he has over a hundred servants. But there's something very human about this handsome man whose favorite course at the university was philosophy. Perhaps he has had to ask deep questions about life because it has not been all that easy. His father died when he was only four. Sent to an English boarding school when he was eight, he returned to India for only a few weeks each year. In many ways he became more English than Indian. He was educated at Eton and Oxford and lived with an English family.

A child of the 60's, he fondly remembers that turbulent, iconoclastic era. "The 60's were an interesting phase of my life," he recalls. "I was given a different perspective and allowed to be an individual."

But his Indian roots reclaimed him from the world of flower children and rebellion. He was called home to assume the mantle of maharaja, a title that even though no longer his legally, was still spiritually valid in traditional Jodhpur.

Singh calls his first couple of years back in Jodhpur "difficult." He saw India as a country of "outmoded ideas and superstitions."

But a visit to England after a few years of living in Jodhpur gave him a new appreciation for India. The maharaja discovered that he had not lost touch with his friends as he had feared.

He also realized that he had not cornered the market on troubles. "Everyone in the university had problems," he remembers. "Seeing that gave me a lot of encouragement." Resolving to put his own life in order, he returned to Jodhpur. He began to appreciate "the strong sense of belonging and responsibility in the clan system."

In 1971 he converted the Umaid Bhawan Palace into a hotel. "People thought I was mad," he chuckles. "There was no tourism to Jodhpur." But the young maharaja had picked up a trick or two from England, where he saw the British making good use of their traditions. Throughout the hotel's history he has honored what he considers worthwhile customs. His hotel is one of the few places where you can see a maharaja holding court. On his birthday some 400 of his clansmen garb themselves in their best Rajput finery and pay respects to their leader.

Known for his kindness, Singh protects his family of servants. Most hotel employees work for Singh, instead of the Welcomgroup chain managing the hotel. Some have been employed by his family for half a century. Described as being solicitous about the welfare of his servants, Singh earlier rejected a management proposal from another chain when the group wanted to bring in their own employees and fire his workers.

A typical day consists of spending the morning tending to mail full of invitations to weddings, seminars, and conferences. Afternoons he meets with press, dignitaries, and hotel guests who have asked to see him. Evenings are for official functions. The maharaja admits he has little private time with his wife, a princess from Poonch, when in Jodhpur. "Sometimes," he admits, "it becomes a bit much." To escape the royal hoopla, the couple travels to Delhi and England.

His biggest difficulty in being a maharaja is having the aura but not the power. Sometimes you're not in the position to do more."

Today the maharaja is involved with nutrition and education projects in a village outside of Jodhpur. He chose to work intensively in a single village rather than superficially in many. He regularly raises money for his charities in England, where people are quite taken with the dark-eyed maharaja. In addition to his duties as maharaja, in 1990 he became a member of parliament, although he says he doesn't like politics. In this role he spearheaded efforts to rebuild Jodhpur's flood damage in the summer of 1990.

Even though he playfully describes his title as an anachronism, the 60's child appears finally to have accepted his role as maharaja. Perhaps he is really speaking of himself when he says, "Maharajas are so intrinsically tied to the people that they cannot tear themselves away from the responsibility of centuries."

Ajit Bhawan

You don't often find a tree growing in your room. Or enter a hotel with a coat rack made from an elephant's trunk. Or discover your closet is a pair of deer antlers. But the Ajit Bhawan has the tree, trunk, antlers, and more. It is one of India's most delightful hotels, an imaginative concoction of whimsy, humor, and a bit of old-fashioned royalty thrown in for good measure. You get the feeling someone had a great time designing its rooms and creating its slightly eccentric, but very warm ambience. If you want to have fun, meet interesting people and feel like part of the family, stay at the Ajit Bhawan. It is owned by Swaroop and Sobhag Singh, uncles of the present maharaja. The quieter Sobhag oversees the garden. The ebullient Swaroop fits in beautifully with the Ajit's wacky atmosphere. He is alternately autocratic, courtly, charming and earthy. But whatever his mood, he makes you feel like family. Retainers fuss over you, keep track of your bill (you never sign anything here), and seem to know all your whims after you've been at the hotel a minute.

The hotel consists of a palace completed by Singh's father in 1935 and adjoining cottages. The stone palace itself is romantic on the outside and filled with dusty antiques on the inside. It houses the reception area, the Singh family's private quarters, and seven standard rooms with high ceilings and old furniture. But more interesting rooms are in the cottages or, as they are known, pavilions. They are sprinkled through beautiful gardens containing tiny bridges, wild parrots, swings, and 150-year-old carriages. You are likely to encounter Sobhag in the garden. He will tell you tales of the way it was before India became democratic. This now very gentle-appearing man was a hunter, but he says hunting in the maharaja days was carefully managed. If you shot a baby or female, your gun was taken away — a great punishment for members of this warrior family.

There are no telephones and television here — just a blackboard outside every cottage on which to scrawl messages for your retainer if you need anything. The hotel provides breakfast in the courtyard, which is best avoided because of the flies, and candlelight dinner in the garden or courtyard. Dinner is served Jodhpur-style in *karwas* (large pots). Ever the gracious hosts, the Singh family mingles with guests. Jodhpur musicians or dancers perform. Guests eat together at common tables. Here you meet your fellow travelers, and a varied lot they are. The more conservative types stay at the Umaid; the adventurous go for the Ajit.

The hotel's rooms — no suites here — are all individually decorated using themes from Jodhpur's villages. The more interesting rooms include: *honeymooners,* number 22, with many large mirrors; *ropemakers,* number 24, with a bathroom made from stones; *hill peoples,* number 26, with a waterfall, a tiger shot by the Singhs' father, and furniture made from deer antlers; *nomad,* number 27, with a tree growing in the room and the bed a converted bullock cart; *agriculture,* number 50, decorated with farm tools; *stone cutter,* number 55, with stone bed and furniture. A not-to-be-missed experience is a desert "safari" with Swaroop, who takes participants to hidden villages. This is a part of India you will not see unless you have a knowledgeable guide like Swaroop. In addition to the inside look at tribal life, you come across spectacular views of desert wildlife. A full-day tour costs approximately $10.

Jodhpur 342 006, Rajasthan, India. Tel. 20409. AE, V. Moderate.

ROYAL AND RUGGED

An outing with Swaroop Singh is never dull. With massive moustaches flying, this descendant of generations of warrior-horsemen drives his jeep as if it were a high spirited steed. The speed of his words equals that of his vehicle as, without pausing, Singh dispenses views on acupressure, the healing properties of cow dung, the environment, Indian politics, and life in general.

His desert "safaris" are a highlight of any Jodhpur visit as much for the opportunity to meet Singh — a combination of courtly maharaja's uncle, go-getting entrepreneur, and downright charmer — as for the chance to see desert villages rarely viewed by tourists.

Years ago Singh, as a member of parliament, became acquainted with Jodhpur area villagers. Today he serves as their unofficial adviser, using his influence to help them in dealings with the government. They in turn open up their homes to him and his little band of tourists. Out of respect for Singh, the peasants treat his strange Westerners with bizarre dress as honored guests.

The maharaja's uncle and the illiterate peasants seem to have developed real affection for each other. Stopping to cuddle a five-year-old whose jewelry indicates she is already married, Singh explains that they regard him as a trusted father. Indeed, the peasants abandon the shyness they usually display around outsiders. A woman whose adobe house the group has just visited stands serenely in front of the tourists, allowing Singh to touch her throat and wrists as he explains how the women's heavy jewelry massages acupressure points. This in a culture that is horrified when a female displays her face before men.

Lake Palace Hotel, Udaipur

Lake Palace Hotel, Udaipur

Sheesh Mahal, flanked by Jahangir and Raja Mahals, Orchha

Lake Palace Hotel, Periyar

Ajit Bhawan, Jodhpur

Further on in another mud hut with thatched roof, in which Singh and the owner have taken a little ritual opium together, a teenage girl appears in shorts. How could she wear such skimpy clothing in front of strangers? She only dresses that way in her home, Singh explains, "and since you are my guests, you are like my family."

The villagers seem to enjoy this father figure as well as respect him. Both men and women banter with him. They laugh often. In turn Singh appears to delight in catching up on the local gossip. His robust voice is heard often, sharing his opinionated views with the villagers very much as he does with the tourists. This Singh is earthy, one who loves speaking the peasants' language. But in a few hours he will transform himself into an elegant, mannerly dinner host, every inch the maharaja's uncle. Although very much a Jodhpurian — "Jodhpur is my shelter, my food, my everything" — much of Singh's life revolves around the West. He runs the Ajit Bhawan, which caters almost entirely to Western tourists, and has sent one of his sons to an American university. His life is very different from what would have been forecast when he was born 14 years before India's independence. In his youth he spent much of his time at the palace with the maharaja's son. He was "very naughty," he admits with a twinkle, "using my muscles when I shouldn't have." He credits an English governess with keeping his high spirits under control.

Singh's mother was in *purdah* and accompanied the Queen Mother of Jodhpur to England, both with body-length umbrellas to enclose them. His wife, too, observed partial *purdah* at first, "but we slowly converted out of *purdah*. In the beginning when you break tradi-

Street art, Udaipur

tion, it feels as if you are breaking a part of yourself."
But Singh is a practical man. "It is necessary to reform
yourself," he says with finality. Full of ideas for making
the rupees roll in, he often sounds like a man with
generations of capitalists, instead of maharajas, in his
blood. His eyes sparkle with life. "I am master of my
appointments, in charge of my own will," he remarks.
Indeed, you feel that this full-spirited man relishes
meeting destiny on its own terms, perhaps as did his
warrior ancestors in battles of long ago.

Khimsar

A popular overnight stop of travelers coming from
Jaipur and going to Jaisalmer, Khimsar is a nondescript desert village whose main attraction is the ruins
of its fifteenth-century castle at the Khimsar Royal
Castle Hotel. It is 125 km from Jodhpur.

Other than the castle, Khimsar is devoid of interesting
sites. However, 10 km west you can find several species
of deer. Nearby is **Khundala,** a thirteenth-century
Hindu temple. Forty km away is the desert city **Nagaur**, known for its cattle fairs in August and February.

Khimsar Royal Castle

The seventeenth-century Mughal emperor Aurangzeb
took two Rajput princes, Zorawar and Bikaner, hostage
to live in his court. When Bikaner became homesick,
Zorawar offered to give the emperor three-quarters of

his territory in Khimsar if Bikaner did not return from a brief visit home. The emperor sanctioned the trip, but Bikaner never returned to the Mughal court. Upholding his end of the agreement, Zorawar offered Khimsar to Aurangzeb. However, the Mughal refused.

Instead, he later stayed at the castle as Zorawar's guest. Although Fateh Mahal, where Aurangzeb slept, is now a ruin, blackened with its centuries of existence, he is still remembered at the castle with a room named in his honor. The castle became a hotel in 1982, but becoming a business seems to have little changed the Khimsar. The sense of the past is strong here; ancestors are honored. Miniature paintings of all 15 generations of the rulers of Khimsar can still be found in the *durbar,* or meeting hall. Swords and guns used to fight the Mughals decorate the lobby.

But the grounds' most historic spot is the grave of the sufi saint Fateh Pir discovered by Khimsar's founder Rao Karam Singji when building the castle in 1423. Rather than removing the shrine, he built his castle beside it and named his palace Fateh Mahal in the saint's honor. You can see Fateh's grave today on the southeast corner of the ruins of Fateh Mahal.

The hulk of Fateh Mahal dominates the hotel. Although only the stone skeleton of what was the castle, it carries a strong energy. The hotel uses it for group dinners lit by bonfires and hurricane lamps. The 12 rooms and suites ($60) are in both an eighteenth-century wing and one built in 1950. Suites are larger with a bit more elaborate decor, but all rooms have old furniture and bedspreads in bright Rajasthani fabrics. Especially outstanding are the miniature paintings from the family's collection in all rooms. Room number 1 in the old wing, the Aurangzeb room, is the most elaborate, with large arches, colored glass and a platform with bolsters for sitting. Rooms in the new wing do not have bathtubs. Only eight rooms are air-cooled.

Although connected with the Welcomgroup, the Khimsar is still owned by the descendants of the original family, who lived in the castle until the 1970's. Today they stay in Jaipur, but visit their property frequently. The hotel is looked after by local people.

Khimsar, Nagaur 341 025, Rajasthan, India. Tel. 28, Khimsar 1-800-223-0888, United States; 44-1-541-1199, London; 0-800-282-811, United Kingdom. Telex 0552-202. No credit cards. Moderate.

Jaisalmer

History says this city in the middle of the Thar desert was founded by an errant Rajput prince. But this, the most magical city in India, seems more like the creation of a fecund storyteller who conjured up Jaisalmer's fort, exquisitely chiseled buildings, and people draped in colors as intense as the desert sun.

Indeed, anything seems possible here except the ordinary. The color of the desert, Jaisalmer shimmers in its sand dunes like a mirage. You keep thinking you will wake up and come back to earth, but you never do. From its warren of lanes to its hidden temples, Jaisalmer is a city of the mysterious, awakening in its visitors the dark area in the human psyche in which myths are born.

You should see everything here because the entire city is colorful. Jaisalmer's heart, its **Fort,** is a maze of winding paths on which you can lose yourself with your dreams. Inside the Fort are wonderfully carved **Jain Temples** dating from the twelfth through fifteenth centuries.

Outside the Fort are *havelis,* gold sandstone mansions sculpted as intricately as wind patterns on desert dunes. The most beautiful is **Patwon-ki-haveli,** five connecting homes built for the sons of a rich trader. It was constructed over a 50-year period starting in 1800.

Nathmal ki Haveli was carved by Muslim brothers who had a contest over who could do the most beautiful work. The results were so extraordinary that neither could be declared the winner. There is a small museum inside.

Salim Sing ki Haveli belonged to a prime minister short on morals but long on artistic taste. Notice the peacock brackets.

Narayan Niwas Palace

When this hotel calls itself a palace, it is stretching the truth. In reality the Narayan Niwas was a caravan-sary, built in 1840 by the maharaja as an inn for traders passing through Jaisalmer.

When the lucrative trade stopped around the time of India's independence in 1947, the caravansary became a school. It was later reclaimed by the royal family and turned into a hotel in 1982. Today it is run by Mohendra Singh, cousin of the maharaja, who is described by a relative as being, in Rajput fashion, "fond of music, women, and wine."

The Narayan's unique lobby eschews its royal heritage in favor of Jaisalmer's folk art. In renovating the lobby and bar, the owners stuck to the design of the original caravansary. Seating is on platforms covered with cushions upholstered in native fabrics. Walls have traditional decorations done by peasant women. Walls, pillars, and arches are plastered in cow dung, which is said to act as a natural insect repellant. The 38 rooms (suites are planned for the future) are basic, with modern, nondescript furniture, except for tables made with Jaisalmer stone. The most interesting room is number 112, which has a bed resting on a sandstone platform.

This nicely run hotel provides Indian dance programs and music at night with meals, which are eaten on the lawn. In addition, it arranges desert tours by jeep or camel. An added bonus is Suman Singh, one of Jaisalmer's best guides, who works out of the Narayan.

Jaisalmer 345 001, Rajasthan, India. Tel. 2408,2397. AE, DC, MC, V. Moderate.

Bikaner

In the middle of the Rajasthan desert, this city was once on a trade route linking eastern India seaports to central Asia. It was conquered by Rajput prince Bika in 1486 and renamed Bikaner.

In the late nineteenth century until 1947 Bikaner was blessed by the rule of Maharaja Ganga Singh. For his time the maharaja was farsighted. He created many public works projects. Bikaner's citizens had reason to be thankful for the ruler's expanding girth during his golden jubilee celebration in 1934. To the chanting of Sanskrit hymns by priests, the maharaja stepped on huge scales. His weight was balanced by gold ingots from his privy purse, which were used for construction of a children's ward at the local hospital.

Junagarh Fort has always protected Bikaner. A huge complex surrounded by a 986-meter-long wall, it was built over a five-year period beginning in 1588. Although attacked, Junagarh was never conquered. Within its thick walls are palaces with such pretty names as Palace of the Moon and Palace of the Flowers. The palaces contain chambers with exquisite frescoes and mosaics that rank with those of Jodhpur Fort and exteriors with fine stone carving. One of its more bizarre features is an ancient airplane resting in a barn-like hall.

The **Shree Sadul Museum** is organized into categories after a fashion, but its sweetness comes from those objects that are in a class of their own. On display are a 100-kilo brass pot used for tax collection, a 1941 census of India, a 1921 film projector still displaying "Made in the USA" in bold letters, old liquor bottles, and a suitcase 6 ft by 4 ft by 8 ft. All items are from the maharaja's collection. The museum is located in the Lallgarh Palace Hotel and makes a stay there more meaningful.

Almost as odd is the government **camel breeding station** located 10 km from town. Possibly the most overworked creatures in all India are the four male camels amongst 160 females. During mating season in the winter the gentlemen mate with five females a day. Considering that it takes camels 45 minutes to have sex, with an additional 10 minutes of foreplay thrown in for good measure, the males are exhausted at the end of the day. The best time to visit the station is late afternoon when the camels come in from grazing.

Lallgarh Palace Hotel

That the 79-year-old manager of the Lallgarh has worked 52 years for the maharaja's family gives you an idea what kind of place this pink sandstone edifice of arches and cupolas is. Senior staff here are loyal retainers of the royal family and run it at the relaxed pace of life more common 50 years ago.

Staying at this 50-room hotel is like being a member of the family. It might take an hour for someone to find the person with the key to the closet containing soap for your bathroom, but the staff is so distressed over your impatience that in the end taking a shower doesn't matter so much. After a day here a friendly smile and good intentions are as pleasing as efficient service.

Designed by Sir Swinton Jacob, architect of Kota's Umaid Bhawan, the four-wing Lallgarh was begun in 1902 during maharaja Ganga Singh's time and finished in 1926. The maharaja is said to have personally selected the furnishings for his palace.

Perhaps some are still in the Lallgarh. Rooms (no suites) are furnished with pieces that have seen better days. Still, for the romantic, they have more character than today's modern ones. Baths are old and large.

Here you can sleep in the bedrooms of the heir apparent and his brother. (One of the two wings which the hotel occupies was lived in by the heir; the other wing was for guests.) Room 102 was the heir's room, room 108 his dressing room. Room 107 was his brother's room, 104 the brother's dressing room.

Halls have what is called "rare" lithographs and etchings. At any rate, they are old and present a view of imperial India. Lounge and dining room feature the typical wooden furniture and animal heads found in many family-run palace hotels.

More interesting is the railroad car parked in front of the hotel. It was the personal car of the Bikaner maharaja. Although now locked, staff will allow you to visit it if you ask. But the building's outstanding feature is in the fourth wing. (The third wing is occupied by the royal family, who are kept from curious guests by protective guards.) Here you will find stone that has been carved into delicate mazes. It is among Rajasthan's most beautiful stonework, and strangely enough is not publicized by the hotel.

An alternative to the Lallgarh is the **Karni Bhavan.**
Built in 1965 by the royal family, this eight-room hotel
was never lived in before it became a hotel. Rooms are
larger and better furnished than the Lallgarh's and go
at slightly lower prices. However, its location is so remote that guests need their own transportation. Also,
the Karni does not have a restaurant. You can, however, take your meals at the Lallgarh.

*Bikaner, Rajasthan, India. Tel. 3263, 5963. No credit
cards. Moderate.*

Jammu & Kashmir

Arguably India's most beautiful state with its mountains, lush valleys, and desert-like plateaus, Jammu and Kashmir has recently been racked with political turmoil in its most touristed area, the **Vale of Kashmir**. Here Muslim militants are agitating for independence from India. Tourist offices are understandably cautious about encouraging visitors to go to Kashmir these days — especially since one Israeli tourist was kidnapped and another killed while trying to escape in 1991. However, travelers still visit Srinagar, the valley's major city, and most find it safe — and more magical than ever because it is now no longer jammed with wall-to-wall tourists. If you are determined to go to the Vale, talk to others who have recently been there and then use your best judgment.

Other than the Vale of Kashmir, Jammu and Kashmir, India's only state with a Muslim majority, has two other distinct geographical areas. The city of **Jammu,** situated where the plains meet the Himalayas, is the headquarters for the southern part of the state. There is a Hindu majority here, with fairly well-known temples.

Then there is the mountainous, dry area of **Ladakh** in the eastern part of the state. Where the mountains surrounding the Vale are green, Ladakh's mountains are barren skeletons of rock which shimmer in browns, mauves, and grays depending on their moods. The people here are Buddhist and come from Tibetan stock. Almost isolated from the twentieth century until twenty years ago, they still retain much of their gentle, childlike character.

With its Himalayas, lakes, and valleys, Jammu and Kashmir is a fine place for trekking. In most places you can hire ponies, porters and gear.

Srinagar

Recently Srinagar has been plagued with political problems. Tourism has plummeted. The many who regard Srinagar as one of the world's most beautiful spots eagerly await the day when freedom will return. In the meantime, check with the Indian tourist office before going.

The romantic meets the hard sell here. Capital of Kashmir, Srinagar lies snuggled in the Himalayas. It is a city of flowers, rainbow sunsets, century-old chinars (a kind of plane tree), and the Dal and Nagin Lakes. It is also a city of super salesmen trailing you around with the ubiquitous mantra, "Madam, please have a look."

The problem is that it is difficult to resist these pesky peddlers, for their wares are often exquisite. Kashmir is above all a sensual land whose products delight the

Jammu & Kashmir

TERU

GILGIT

HAJI LANGAR

CHILAS

MUZAFFARADAD

BARAMULA

SRINAGAR

GULMARG

PAHALGAM

LEH

PUNCH

PULWAMA

ANANTNAG

RIASI

MIRPUR

1A

AKHNUR

JAMMU

CHUMAR

hand and eye. Her craftspeople produce shawls so fine
they can be drawn through a ring and rugs that take a
year to weave.

Mainly travelers enjoy Srinagar's natural sites by being
rowed around her lakes in *shikaras,* the Kashmiri gon-
dola with plump cushions and heart-shaped paddles.
By *shikara* you can go under her nine bridges, pass by
gabled houses, and encounter Kashmiris hawking
honey and saffron.

But Srinagar has her share of historical sites as well:
the 400-year-old **Jami Masjid** mosque, an equally old
Hindu temple on Shankaracharya Hill; and the Mughal
gardens **Nishat, Nasim,** and **Shalimar.** In addition,
excursions to nearby **Gulmarg** and **Pahalgam,** mountain villages of rivers and meadows, give you the Hima-
lyas' full majesty.

The Oberoi Palace

The facade of the Oberoi seems almost austere when
compared to other palaces' curlicues and cupolas. The
hotel is an unadorned rectangular structure, at first
appearing more institutional than palatial.

But the Oberoi grows on you because it is a building
that blends with nature rather than competing with
her. This 20-acre estate includes fruit trees and enormous dahlias, two very old chinar trees, and views of
the lake and mountains.

Maharaja Hari Singh designed the palace in the late
1920's. Later Singh was criticized for his indecisive-

ness in being unable to decide whether to make Kashmir a part of Pakistan or India after Independence. (In all fairness to the maharaja, it was a tough decision. Singh was Hindu, while most of his constituents were Muslim.)

The palace hints at the maharaja's character. According to his grandson Yuvraj Vikramadmitya Singh, Hari wanted "something simple, something to blend with the environment." The palace's clean lines were perhaps an antidote to the shy maharaja's unhappy childhood filled with dangerous byzantine intrigue.

Hari lived there until 1948. At that time a forest grew almost to the palace's backyard. Hari once shot a panther from the front lawn. Another maharaja killed a bear from his bathroom. The house was filled with parties and guests. The British Viceroy visited once a year and stayed in what is now the Presidential Suite ($270). Louis Mountbatten arrived to hurry along Singh's decision on Kashmir's fate after independence, but the maharaja kept him so busy with festivities that he had little time for political talks with the recalcitrant maharaja. Gandhi also visited here. During the summer the Indian princes arrived with their retinues for a season of polo playing.

But politics did not allow Hari to attain the palace's promise of peace. After Indian independence he was exiled to Bombay, never to return to his home of mountains and flowers.

Today the palace offers the serenity that Hari Singh sought. Now leased by the Oberoi, which added another wing, it is a genteel reminder of its former glory. Furniture has been kept in the European style popular during Singh's era. Many of the Kashmiri carpets are threadbare in places. They are genuine artifacts from palace days and are now more beautiful in their old age. Even though the pile has worn down, so fine is rugmaking in Kashmir that the weave will last indefinitely.

Service is friendly but slow. Yet no one seems to mind the wait. Time becomes less important against this backdrop of mountains and lake.

Former prime minister Rajiv Gandhi stayed here regularly when he was an Indian Airlines pilot and his mother was prime minister. During one of his visits a feisty Kashmiri cab driver decided Gandhi had insulted him and deposited Rajiv and his suitcases at the bottom of the long drive leading to the hotel.

"I don't care who you are," the cab driver is said to have snapped. "If you insult me, you're going to walk." Rajiv walked.

The former quarters of the maharaja and maharani have sitting rooms with Kashmiri carpets, furniture belonging to the royal family, and marble fireplaces. Views include both mountain and lake. The doors are palace era. Bathrooms have elderly fixtures and are in marble.

The hotel has three deluxe suites ($170) and 20 standard suites ($90). The standard suites 205-209 and 215-219 with lake views do not have dressing rooms. There are also 36 standard rooms. In the new wing all rooms face the garden and are smaller. The old wing's rooms have more character, but some do not have views.

The hotel serves a buffet in the evenings with both Western and Indian food. In summer most people eat lunch on the lawn under the chinar trees and enjoy the lake view.

Available activities include mini golf course and badminton courts. Horseback riding, trekking, and water sports can be arranged.

Srinagar 190 001. Tel. 71241-2, India; 1-800-223-1474, United States; 44-81-788-2070, United Kingdom. Telex 201. AE, DC, MC, V. Very expensive.

Uttar Pradesh

UTTARKASHI

RAURI

MUZAFFARNAGAR

RISHIKESH ALMORA

HARDWAR PITHORAGARH

BIJNOR

DELHI

24

ALIGARH

ETAH LAKHIMPUR

AGRA

2

LUCKNOW

AYODHYA

UNAIAG SULTANPUR

FATEHPUR

29

ORAI

2 VARANASI

BANDA BALLIA

ORCHHA

MIRZAPUR

Uttar Pradesh

You feel that you are in eternal India in Uttar Pradesh, the country's most densely populated state. Here bullock carts still plow the fertile farmlands, and many villagers rarely leave their villages. Although large, cities are sleepy with more rickshaws than taxis.

It is also a state in which the Hindu heart beats strongly. Seemingly eternal, **Varanasi,** India's holiest city, is located in UP, as it is called, and the Ganges, her most sacred river, flows through the state, washing away ignorance and allowing worshippers to begin anew. Believers, ranging from simple people to naked holy men, also flock to the state's other religious centers, **Hardwar** and **Rishikesh.**

This is also the state where prejudices are as ancient as its sites. Colonized by Muslim Mughal emperors in the sixteenth and seventeenth centuries, the state has a large Muslim population. Although Muslims and Hindus lived together peacefully until the British pitted the two groups against each other to further British aims, the state has been marked by clashes between members of both religions. Recently the two have squared off in a dispute over whether a structure in Ayodhya should be a temple or mosque. The issue was important in the fall of one national government and the formation of another one.

India's main tourist attraction, the **Taj Mahal** in Agra, is also located in the state. Constructed by emperor Shah Jahan as a monument to his wife in 1653, the Taj is a living structure, changing colors during different times of the day and eliciting strong emotions. This 300-year-old monument to love still manages to create a reverence for the beauty of the human spirit in those who view it today. It is well worth braving the hard-edged, heavily-touristed Agra for a visit.

Lucknow

Although the capital city of India's most important state, Uttar Pradesh, Lucknow seems far from the power plays of Indian politics. With its sleepy tempo and crumbling old mansions, it whispers of the aristocratic age of the nawabs of Oudh, who ruled the city during the eighteenth and nineteenth centuries. In Lucknow you are likely to meet many of their descendants, who have lost their wealth, but not their old world manners.

As India's principal Shi'ite Muslim city, Lucknow is the home of architecturally distinct *imambaras,* tombs for Shi'ites. The **Great Imambara** has one of the largest vaulted halls in the world. Built in 1784, it is a maze of passages. The many-domed **Hussainabad Imambara** was constructed in 1837 as a massive public works project. It houses the tomb of nawab Muhammad Ali Shah. This nawab also began construction of the **Jami Masjid** mosque. This large structure is not open to non-Muslims.

Reminding that Lucknow is a political city as well as spiritual one is the **Residency,** which witnesssed the heart of the Indian rebellion against the British in the 1857 mutiny. Here British troops were holed up for 87 days defending against the Indians. Today the Residency has been kept eerily the same as it was during the last days of the fighting. The walls are still scarred with gunshot, and the cemetery bears the remains of 2,000 English who were killed during the rebellion.

Carlton Hotel

With a stuffed, snarling tiger standing over mothballs, a dusty deer head, a portrait of a young Indira Gandhi, a senile switchboard, and a few wicker-and-leatherette chairs strewn around as an afterthought, the Carlton's lobby perfectly captures the ambience of decline that permeates this hotel. The Carlton's decline is that of the aristocrat, who gently clings to the dusty artifacts of richer times.

Although never a palace, this rambling two-story rust and ivory structure of domes and arches has hosted Queen Elizabeth and a medley of maharajas, many of whom rented entire wings. It was built in 1890 by Britisher Charles Lincoln, who brought in an English architect. But instead of creating a very proper English edifice, the architect fell in love with Lucknow's architecture and designed a whimsical building incorporating the Moghul, Gothic, and Gallic styles of Lucknow buildings. The Carlton would be the model for later government hostels.

During its first years the hotel served as a guesthouse for British officers. The class-conscious British would not allow Indians to walk along the road fronting the Carlton. After 1921 Lincoln allowed Indian maharajas to stay there. They came with a retinue of 50 servants, who were housed in tents set up on the hotel's large grounds. Later the hotel was the favored hangout of Indian politicians — the homespun-clad Congress politicians spurned the Carlton at first as being too opulent, but growing accustomed to life's finer things accompanying power, soon relented. American and English soldiers used to have fist fights over women here during World War II. Most of India's top leaders, from Nehru to his daughter Indira Gandhi, have at one time slept at the Carlton.

In 1944 the war claimed both of Charles Lincoln's sons. Deeply depressed, he sold the Carlton to the Singh family and returned to England, where he gave the profits from the sale to the British war effort. The Singhs did away with the hotel's big man-pulled fans and installed the latest innovation, electric ceiling fans. Another technological wonder were the electrical buzzers — still in the rooms today — to summon servants. Later the Singhs lowered the Carlton's 25-ft ceilings to install central air conditioning.

Today the hotel seems at least 50 years behind the times. If efficiency and cleanliness are important to you, stay away. Servants move in slow motion. Sheets are often not changed daily. Your clothes come back from the laundry a different color from when they went in.

But if you are after soul, or spirit, or whatever we call that elusive quality that technology often quashes, head for the Carlton. The world's slowest servants lack finesse, but they might give you flowers at the end of your stay. The waiters will go out of their way to sneak you your favorite dishes. You will meet Peter, a 91-year-old waiter, who owner Yogandra Singh says is his most prompt employee. Peter retired at 65, but in two weeks was back at the hotel, telling Singh, "If you retire me, pick up a gun and shoot me." Peter got his job back and has been charming guests ever since. Indeed, the Carlton's 120-person staff is a family, many of whom live on the hotel's 10 acres and have worked for the hotel for several generations. As with any family, you have to take the good along with the bad. What they lack in efficiency, they make up for in their acceptance of guests not as bearers of rupees, but as human beings.

Along with its colorful employees, the Carlton's other charm is its garden. With flowering flame trees, abundant bird life, and the Singh family's army of animals ranging from Great Danes and golden retrievers to geese, it is a nature lover's delight. There is a wide arc of lawn in front of the hotel, from which you sip cold drinks in the evening. Also belonging to another era, the hotel's 100 rooms are slightly run down at the edges. They have large windows and glass-paned doors. Although it is supposedly difficult to see inside the rooms during the day, those with a penchant for privacy might find the feeling of living in a glass house disconcerting. Furnishings are nondescript. Cottages ($64) include two bedrooms, dining room, kitchen, and sitting room. The hotel also has a restaurant, bar, and small shops.

Shahnajaf Road, Lucknow 226 001. Tel. 44021-4. Telex 0535-7217. AE, DC, MC. Inexpensive.

Madhya Pradesh

BHIND

ORCHHA GWALIOR

③

TIKAMGARH • PANNA
KHAJURAHO
SIDHI
MANDSAUR • RAJGARH
• SANCHI ㉖ ⑦
RATLAM • BHOPAL
UJJAIN AMBIKAPUR
⑫
MANDLA
BILASPUR
CHHINDWARA
RAIPUR
DURG ⑥
KHARGON
RAJ NANDGAON
DHAMTARI
MANPUR
㊸
JAGDALPUR

Madhya Pradesh

India's largest state, Madhya Pradesh is located in the country's heart. Meaning the "middle state," Madhya ranges from flatlands to rivers to forests — in fact, this state contains nearly one-third of India's woodlands.

It also offers a variety of attractions for travelers. In the north, **Gwalior,** once one of the wealthier princely states, maintains its old fort and palace. Another example of royal India is the deserted medieval city of **Orchha.**

Further south, made infamous by the deadly release of poisonous gas from the Union Carbide plant, the capital of the state, **Bhopal**, mixes ugly industries with mosques and palaces.

Nearby is **Sanchi,** now a small town, but once a Buddhist center. Its stupas still stun travelers.

The awesome Hindu temples at **Khajuraho** are world famous. Dating from the tenth through the eleventh centuries, these temples are covered with erotic sculptures. Scholars can only surmise why they were built. Some suspect they were a form of tantric worship. Others think they were meant to instruct on sexuality. Whatever the reason, they remain one of India's outstanding sights.

Gwalior

Three-and-a-half hours south of Delhi by India's fastest train (the *Shatabdi Express)*, in the state of Madhya Pradesh, this mid-sized Indian city is not a must on most tourist circuits. You will find its old streets refreshingly free of tourists, its pace dictated by citizens rather than visitors.

Atop a steep rocky hill, its **fort** — one of India's best — dates from at least the fourteenth century. As you ascend, you will notice giant Jain sculptures carved from the rock. The fort's centerpiece is **Man Singh Palace,** which still has tiles with turquoise ducks and elephants decorating the exterior. In one of the palace's two underground levels you can see where the women awaited word of their men's victory or defeat and the pit in which they would burn themselves if their armies were defeated. The palace was built in the late fifteenth century.

Also on fort grounds is **Teli-ka-Mandir,** or Honeymoon Temple. Embellished with fine sculptures, this ninth-century temple dates from a time in which India was not puritanical about sex. It was supposedly used to instruct young couples on the arts and duties of marriage.

Other temples are eleventh-century **Sasbahu,** or Mother-in-Law and Daughter-in-Law temples. This is India and so, of course, the Mother-in-Law is larger and more beautiful. In the new town is the **Jai Vilas Palace,** the palace of the last maharaja. A visit to this palace shows you how every royal attic must have looked. Its clutter of objects that once must have appeared exotic is almost overwhelming.

Gwalior also has one of the best guides in India. Yashwant Singh's father lived at the fort and worked for the British. Singh has lived at the fort all of his life. He has absorbed its spirit as well as countless stories that you won't find in books. This guide who has shown luminaries such as Benazir Bhutto around Gwalior is both a masterful story teller and teacher. You can contact him through the Usha Kiran Palace.

Usha Kiran Palace

Flanked by twin towers, this white-and-butterscotch palace was built in 1902 to house guests for the Prince of Wales' visit. It is near the Jai Vilas Palace. After the prince was gone, as the European Guest House, it continued its role of housing visiting Europeans.

In the '40s Maharaja Madho Rao Scindia turned the structure into a residence for his son and four daughters. After the maharaja's death, his widow Vijaya Raja and his son engaged in one of those ancestral quarrels that has split many an Indian royal family. Two of the sisters sided with the mother, two with the brother. Mother and son formally parted in 1975 with each getting half of the estate. Vijaya has become active in Indian politics. One of the leaders of the conservative Hindu revivalist BJP party, she was arrested in 1990 demonstrations. However, her longest stint in jail was under Indira Gandhi. Her son, on the other hand, became a member of the Congress Party and served as

Minister of Railways under Rajiv Gandhi and Minister of Tourism in the P.V. Narasimha Rao government. Neither has much contact with the hotel, which joined the Welcomgroup chain in 1987.

The Usha Kiran has kept many of its ties with the past. The carved rosewood elevator with original glass dates from 1930. Two-blade ceiling fans also are from palace days. A billiard table in one of the conference rooms was perfectly preserved until a few years ago when a drunken tourist tore it.

All 27 rooms are different, furnished with both new and nicely preserved old furniture. They are beautifully maintained. Rooms 22-25 were part of the *zenana.* Room 23 contains mirrorwork in the dressing room as well as stone carvings. Room 26 has its original red oriental carpet and art deco furniture. If you want to sleep in the room of a prince or princess, go for rooms 28-31, part of the master bedroom; or 20-21 and 32-33, the rooms of the four sisters. Suite 21 ($83) has king-sized rooms with art deco furniture and tri-colored stone floor.

The hotel's grounds with fountains and lawns invite sipping a sunset drink and gazing up at the carved stone panels, each with its individual design, on the palace's facade.

Jayendraganj, Lashkar, Gwalior 474 009, Madhya Pradesh. Tel. (0751)23453, (0751)22049. Cable USHAKIRAN. AE, DC, MC, V. Expensive.

Orchha

Nestled in hills 18 km from Jhansi, Orchha is an eighteenth-century city of ruins. Overgrown with weeds and blackened with time, her aging palaces speak of both human beings' glory and their frailty.

Dauji ki Kothi lies crumbling in a bed of weeds. **Jahangir Mahal,** with latticed windows, sculpted vaults, and turquoise tiles, is a maze of courtyards, tiny rooms, and hidden stairs. The three-story structure offers views of this kingdom of ruins. You are often joined by resident hawks and vultures who fly close to the building's upper floors. In the **Raja Mahal** the colonnaded *durbar,* or meeting hall, has ceiling frescoes now almost destroyed by the passage of the years.

Sheesh Mahal

Linking the Jahangir and the Raj Mahal is the Madhya Pradesh Tourist Development Corp's Sheesh Mahal. Instead of allowing it to show off graceful aging like its sister buildings, some tidy soul has whitewashed the outer structure, divesting it of much of its character. The Sheesh Mahal was built in 1763 by the Orchha maharaja as a rest house. Today its lobby, with lines of yellow stucco arches and an army of ceiling fans, is a cool retreat from Orchha's midday sun. Doubling as a restaurant, the lobby is a popular luncheon spot for the area's daytime visitors. Five of the hotel's six rooms open from the lobby. With vaulted ceilings, peeling paint, and ugly modern furniture, all rooms are similar. The establishment's pride is its one air-conditioned room which is larger than the others and has somewhat nicer furnishings.

The manager is unable to give even the most basic information on the Sheesh Mahal's history, but will supply a book detailing the area's past on request. In many ways, however, you don't need a book to capture the drama of empire and kings. With Orchha's ruins everywhere you look, the Sheesh Mahal brings the past into the present.

Orchha, Dist. Tikam Garh, Madhya Pradesh, India. Tel. 224. No credit cards. Inexpensive.

Gujarat

This western state is the home of both one of India's most ancient archaeological sites and one of her greatest industrial cities. It has witnessed the ascetic Mahatma Gandhi, who was born there, and the money-minded traders for which it is famous. It is the scene of India's most stringent dry laws and one of her most fun-loving islands where booze flows freely.

Gujarat's beginnings date back some 3,500 years to **Lothal,** an archaeological site which can be visited today. Nearby is the noisy, crowded modern city of **Ahmedabad** with its many textile mills. It is a city of mosques and "step wells," with steps leading into the earth. Here you will find the *pols,* dead-end streets once built for defense but now mere alleys jammed with architecturally interesting structures. This bustling state known for its aggressive traders also played a major role in Gandhi's life. He was born in Porbandar and went to school in Bhavnagar. In Ahmadabad is **Sabarmati Ashram,** which he founded in 1918. But Gujarat has an international flavor as well as an Indian one. Although technically a union territory (and thus exempt from Gujarat's dry laws), the island of **Diu** is in the southern part of the state. A Portuguese territory until 1961, Diu is an island of sandy beaches, cliffs, an old fort, and booze It is a favorite of Gujaratis escaping the state's no-liquor laws.

Other worthwhile sites include **Palitana,** with its hilltop collection of 863 Jain temples, and the **Sasan Gir Lion Sanctuary,** the only place in India where the Indian lion still lives.

Bhavnagar

On the Gulf of Cambay in the western state of Gujarat, this port city is notable as the site where Gandhi spent some of his student years. Tourists often stay here enroute to the Jain hillside pilgrimage spot **Palitana** 56 km away, or to the ruins of **Lothal**, the civilization of 4,500 years ago, some 70 km from Bhavnagar.

The **Gandhi Smriti,** a library and photo gallery featuring pictures from Gandhi's life, is well worth a visit. Here photos and correspondence — including letters exchanged with Leo Tolstoy — are arranged chronologically. By the time you finish viewing the exhibit, you are under the great man's gentle spell. Bhavnagar's other site is the **Takhteshwar Temple,** a small Shiva temple of white carved marble atop a hill.

Hotel Nilambag Palace

The Bhavnagar maharajas eschewed the flash beloved by most of their royal cousins. Their 125-year-old stone palace lined with a series of stepped, pointed pseudo-arches, more reminiscent of Rome than flamboyant

Lallgarh Palace Hotel, Bikaner

Lalitha Mahal Hotel, Mysore

Maharaja's Palace, Mysore   *Lallgarh Palace Hotel, Bikaner (right)*

India, reflects their understated good taste. Not that the Nilambag is without drama. Gujarat is known for its wood carving, and the carved teak in the hotel entrance is among the state's finest. In the lobby are king-size paintings of the royal family and a still-lovely 100-year-old carpet. A rosewood chest holds an elderly phonograph, and a pot of red water is there to bring good luck.

The 14 standard rooms and two suites in the three-story structure surround a courtyard containing a single brass water fountain. You reach upper floors via a 100-year-old teak elevator or a winding teak staircase.

Suites ($28) and rooms contain old furniture either from the maharaja's collection made by local craftsmen or new furniture done in the old style. All standard rooms here are sizable; many contain dressing rooms as large as standard hotel rooms. All are beautifullly maintained.

The most interesting suite is 203, where the maharani once stayed. Entered by doors with silver handles, it has a fine carved wood headboard and its own private balcony. The bathroom is so large you could get lost.

Also notable is the third floor hall's rosewood swing.

The Nilambag sits on 15,841 sq meters of gardens and other buildings owned by the maharaja. Here you can walk amongst old trees and enjoy abundant bird life.

The maharaja's home is on the same grounds near the swimming pool (which is not available for guests). Part

Lalitha Mahal Hotel, Mysore

Gujarat

PALANPUR

MAHESANA

15

BHUJ

8

SURENDRANAGAR

GANDHINAGAR

AHMEDABAD

8A

KHEDA

BHAVNAGAR

88

PALITANA

AMRELI

JUNAGADH

BHARUCH

SURAT

DIU

AHWA

of the Welcomgroup chain, the hotel is owned by the royal family. It is managed much more efficiently than most family-owned palace hotels.

Because of Gujarat's dry laws, imbibers beware. Booze is not available here. But you can sip your soft drinks in the garden bar which is open in the evenings from 6:30 to 11:30.

Bhavnagar 364 002, Gujarat, India. Tel. 29323, 21337, Bhavnagar; 1-800-223-0888, United States; 44-1-541-1199, United Kingdom. AE, DC, MC, V. Moderate.

THE GENTLE MAHARAJA

Dr. Virbhadra Singhji K. Gohil would be Bhavnagar maharaja if maharajas still officially existed. He is at once shy and warm in his greeting, like an unspoiled child.

Moustached, with a cane he uses for a limp resting at his side, he sits sipping a soft drink in the lobby of his hotel, the Nilambag Palace. Gohil, 58, erects few of the walls around himself which other maharajas frequently use when giving interviews. He answers questions without guile, laughing frequently, again much like a child, simultaneously vulnerable and wise.

He was born here on the second floor. The Bhavnagar rulers were advanced for their times. Gohil says his grandmother was the first court woman to reject *purdah* nearly 100 years ago. Pride creeps into his voice as he explains his father was the first maharaja to give up his rights. He remembers his father receiving Gandhi during the heady days of India's independence movement.

However, Gohil was not overly conscious of political life during the first years of his country's independence. Mostly he concentrated on his education. He went to school at Bhavnagar University "to get in touch with the local people." He says he had friends over to his home — no matter that it was the local palace — like a normal university student, but you get the feeling that this gentle man probably doesn't know exactly what normal folks do. Still, his warmth, if not his title, must have made him somewhat accessible to his fellow students.

Later he transferred to Bombay University, where he earned his Ph.D in sociology, a subject that appeals to him because it allows you "to study the psychological approach toward life." He wrote his dissertation on "The Social Organization of Rajputs in Saurashtra." A Rajput himself, he interviewed many of this warrior class while working on his Ph.D. He found his own intimate knowledge of the clan useful. "They would tell me they did one thing," he laughs, "and I knew they really did the opposite."

He himself never seems to have identified with the Rajput machismo. His main interests are painting — he works with water colors — and playing the sitar. "We artists are quite half mad," he confides. He also advises sociology students on their doctoral theses.

Gohil lives with his wife on the hotel grounds in a separate house. The couple also spends much of their time in Bombay. With the abolition of the maharajas' privy purse in 1971, he says his family felt the financial crunch. He had to stop educating local children, and he turned the Nilambag into a hotel.

How does he feel about the lobby's stuffed tiger, the victim of a royal hunt? "I only put it here because people expect animal trophies." He chuckles sweeetly. "Personally I would rather paint animals, or keep them as pets."

Andhra Pradesh

Andhra Pradesh

This pleasant southern state has few tourist attractions — perhaps a plus for those who like their sites full of local people and empty of tourists. People here are friendly and living is cheap, making Andhra the perfect stopover between serious sightseeing excursions.

The capital, **Hyderabad,** is an important repository of Muslim history and monuments. Southeast of Hyderabad are the ruins of a **Buddhist center** that flourished from 200 BC to 300 AD.

The final Andhra site is **Tirumala,** one of India's pilgrimage spots. Here non-Hindus are permitted into the temple, but the long lines to receive a blessing leave you feeling tired rather than spiritually renewed.

Hyderabad

This capital of Andhra Pradesh combines both Muslim and Hindu influences. Even though it has a population well over three million, there is something of the village bazaar here perhaps because of its sizable Muslim population. Here in the city center you will find men hawking Mideastern bread, boys pounding silver leaf which will become a line from the Koran written in

Arabic, and shops selling both framed verses from the Koran and pictures of the Hindu teacher Maha Yogini. Veiled Muslim women peer at gaudy plastic bangles.

Before independence Hyderabad was once the principality of what was perhaps the world's richest man. Ruling a population 85% Hindu, the Muslim Nizam was a colorful, if not very pleasant character. Smoking the native hand-rolled cigarette *bidis,* he was adept at bumming the more expensive variety from visitors. He was said to smoke cigarette stubs from ashtrays. The miserly ruler stored much of his wad in his palace, where it was eventually forgotten and lost to nibbling rats.

In the old city two must-sees stand close to each other. The graceful arch **Charminar** built by Muhammed Quli Qutab Shah in 1591 is the city's symbol. Nearby is the **Mecca Masjid,** one of the world's largest mosques. Built in the seventeenth century, it is a peaceful place with a spacious courtyard and cool marble tombs.

The **Salar Jang Museum** is an eccentric collection of everything from carpets to crystal to costumes that once belonged to a Hyderabad prime minister. The gentleman never threw anything away. You can spend an entire morning viewing the 35,000 items constituting his effects.

But Hyderabad's most interesting sites are 11 km out of town. The **Golconda Fort** marked the region's capital until 1590. Later it saw action when Hyderabad's rulers battled the Mughals. Mostly ruins today, its thick walls and superb acoustics (you can hear a word spoken at the bottom of the fort all the way at the top 120 meters away) are impressive.

Close by are the **Qutab Shahi** kings' tombs. These are beautiful structures with fat rounded domes and fine stonework.

Ritz Hotel

This venerable old lady of a hotel has grown a bit frayed around the edges. Once Hyderabad's only decent hotel, it has since been topped by new Taj and Oberoi hotels. Still, outwardly at least, it remains an impressive site, sparkling white with towers shaped somewhat like those in European castles and surrounded by five acres of grounds and gardens. Before it became a hotel in 1956 it was the Hill Fort Palace, residence of Princess Neilofer, daughter-in-law of the Nizam. The structure was built in 1936.

The princess' room is now one of the hotel's rather dull suites. (No one knows where her husband's rooms were.) Number 11, it consists of a large sitting room done in mostly modern furniture, but some pieces such as a couch with carved rosewood edges and a rosewood cabinet with silver handles are old. Her original tub is in the bathroom, surrounded by mirrors, one of which is broken. The soap dish, said to be the one belonging to Neilofer, is the ugliest one in India.

The 33 standard rooms are all wall papered and furnished with castoff '50s pieces. The pool here is large and downhill from the hotel. The dining room has no ambience, but it does have a quirky Western band composed of Indian musicians.

Management seems to be wanting. For instance, the bar's centerpiece is an enormous picture of a little dog pulling down a beautiful woman's panties. But the staff is friendly and helpful. If you stay for a few days, you will surely walk away with some friends.

Hill Fort Palace, Hyderabad 500 463, Andhra Pradesh, India. Tel. (0842)233571. Telex 0425-6215. AE, DC, MC, V. Expensive.

Karnataka

Karnataka once saw empires rise and fall. The Hoysalas ruled between the eleventh and fourteenth centuries. Reaching its apex in the sixteenth century, the Vijayanagar was one of India's most important governments. Later Tipu Sultan fought a brave but losing battle against the British. The last ruler to lead Karnataka was the maharaja of Mysore, whose kingdom was one of the wealthiest of the princely states.

The bloody power struggles have disappeared, but all the empires left their monuments in Karnataka. The Hoysalas bequeathed **Belur** and **Halebid,** star-shaped temples covered with exquisite sculpture — some of it erotic. The Vijayanagars left us a temple at **Hampi** which is a World Heritage Monument. At Srirangapatnam are the remains of **Tipu's capital**. Finally, the maharaja's opulent palace is in Mysore.

Other sites worth a visit in this state, where women wear jasmine in their hair and bullocks' horns are decorated, include one of the most important Jain temples. High on its own hill, **Sravanabelagola** gives you a good workout in reaching the top. It is crowned by a statue of Lord Bahubali, the world's tallest monolithic statue.

Karnataka's capital, **Bangalore** is one of the country's fastest growing cities. It has become a center for high tech industry.

Mysore

In the southern Indian state of Karnataka, this pleasant city has women sporting jasmine in their long black hair, bullocks with painted horns, and sandalwood incense wafting through the air.

The city's rose-colored **Maharaja's Palace** could be from Disneyland, but actually is the king's home. Built in 1907, it has all the flash and pomp of princely India with carved ceilings, cool marble, and chambers decked out in their finest. It also has a museum with paintings of the current maharaja's ancestors. Another site is 1,000 (at least) steps up Chamundi Hill. Here rests a **Shiva temple** with a 40-meter-high tower. On the way up you will see the five-meter-high **Nandi,** Shiva's bull, carved out of a single piece of rock. Also colorful is the **Devaraja vegetable market** with men selling tiny pyramids of powder in every color imaginable and women hawking tropical fruits.

Ashok Radisson Lalitha Palace Hotel

What does one do with polluting guests who eat meat, drink alcohol, and soak in tubs, instead of showering? If you're the Mysore maharaja, you build them their own palace.

Constructed in 1921 by Maharaja Krishna Rajendra Wodeyar to house his European guests, the white stucco Lalitha Mahal must have provided breathing space for both cultures. Here the Europeans could imbibe and eat all the meat they wanted, and the maharaja could be considered the gracious host.

European dignitaries stayed here frequently on their journeys from Bangalore to Ooty. As befitting its Western heritage, the Lalitha has never known an Indian-style toilet. Even today in the Vicereine Suite the toilet is marked "Shank & Co, Barehead, Scotland," certifying its proper lineage.

After independence the maharaja pared his budget, cutting down on entertainment. He turned the Lalitha over to the government, which from 1955 to 1972 used it as a government guest house. It became part of the government-run Indian Tourist Development Corp. in 1974. The ITDC added a new wing in the 1970s.

Star suites are the Viceroy and Vicereine ($415). The Vicereine has teak and ebony woods, gold velvet furnishings, and marble light fixtures. Even though designed for the European look then in vogue, the dressing table displays its Indian heritage with numerous drawers for bangles and nose rings. Note the royal insignia, the double-headed eagle, on the mirror and light fixtures.

The Viceroy features turquoise furniture, four-poster bed, and silk curtains. It includes a curious contraption with places for gentlemen to hang their coats, hats, pants, ties, and walking sticks — and wheels on which servants could roll it out of the room.

Old wing standard rooms with high ceilings and Victorian furniture are for the romantically-minded. New wing rooms are modern with small balconies. A step down in size, they are about the dimensions of an old wing bathroom. All have swimming pool views.

Public rooms capture the feel of raj India. Pictures of former maharajas are at staircase landings. You can see British influence creeping into princely India with the Victorian stars one ruler displays on his chest. Notice in the painting of Sri Krishna Raja Wodeyar how the maharaja's eyes and shoes seem to follow the viewer from any direction. Also noteworthy because it comes from the palace is the rosewood table under the paintings. In the bar the snooker table and liquor cabinets are also original.

For fun Europeans used to gather in the banquet hall, which is now the old-fashioned dining room. They were entertained with nightly music. Acoustics in the cavernous chamber were so perfect that performers did not need a microphone.

On Sunday evenings the Maharaja's Palace is lit up and visible from the Lalitha. The maharaja had the Lalitha designed so that it could be seen from his meeting hall at the palace. Their bond seems strongest on Sunday evenings. At that time you can almost see Europeans and Indians gazing out at each other's quarters and hear them gossiping about the other's strange ways.

Mysore 570011, India. Tel. 26316,27650, and 27771. Telex 0846-217. AE, DC, MC, V. Very Expensive.

Tamil Nadu

Because it often remained untouched by the waves of light-skinned invaders that swept across northern India, Tamil Nadu is frequently called the most Indian state. Its citizens are gentle and religious. In fact, so religious that temples with *gopurams,* the characteristic Tamil Nadu-style tower, lushly decorate the area. The state includes major pilgrimage centers, most of which are not open to non-Hindus. One of the most dramatic temples is the one at **Mahabalipuram,** which is on the shore and is a World Heritage Monument. Tamil Nadu's capital, **Madras,** is South India's major city. With its mementos from the British raj era, the city offers fairly interesting sights. Also noteworthy is **Pondicherry,** a former French settlement, with the **Sri Aurobindo Ashram,** one of the India's most important spiritual centers. When temple hopping gets to be a bit much, you can head for the hill stations in the Nilgiri Hills for cool weather and a spot of nature.

Ootacamund (Ooty)

Known as Snooty Ooty from its days as the summer headquarters of the British, this hill station in the south Indian state of Tamil Nadu is famous for its weather and views. When all India is sweltering, Ooty is cool — as it should be at 2,200 meters above sea level. Conversely, when India is cool, Ooty is freezing — which explains why prices dip sharply during the winter and monsoon seasons.

As for views, they are green and lush. With its stone churches and crumbling cottages punctuating green hills and valleys, this dowager city invites long walks. This is a place to relax. But, aside from enjoying nature, there isn't much else to do.

Fernhill Palace

The location of this rust and white, tile-roofed hotel couldn't be more scenic. On 50 acres of rolling lawns and gardens surrounded by Ooty's hills, this rambling structure feels like an overgrown country house. Which it was. Built 125 years ago, it was the Mysore maharaja's summer palace. No matter that he constructed the huge structure to live in only a couple of weeks of the year when Mysore's heat became too much. For the maharajas life was lavish with possibilities.

It is still in the family, now owned by his grandson, Narasimaraja Wodeyar, who spends even less time than his ancestor here.

The Fernhill has the charm of an old hotel. The teak-paneled lobby is decorated with the heads of animals unfortunate enough to be downed in a *shikara,* or royal hunt. Once the banquet room, the high-ceilinged restaurant also has its share of teak. Ironically this ornate room with balcony and chandeliers was designed for country living. Still, there is a feel of the country in the light, bright halls lined with one wall of French windows. Each of the 47 rooms is different, and each one makes you feel you are stepping back in time to a more elegant era. All contain items from the Mysore palace. Since the building has no central heating, every room is equipped with a working fireplace — useful for warding off Ooty's monsoon and winter chill.

Rooms are classified as standards and deluxe. One of the nicest standards is 118, with glass-enclosed entryway, small sitting room, and huge cupboard. Avoid rooms 209-216, which are small. Number 103 is the hotel's best deluxe. Done in orange, it has tiles adorning the fireplace, teak floors, and a roomy bath.

Away from the main building, in what was the servants' quarters, are 17 cottages which go for half the price of palace rooms. They don't have the ambience of the other rooms, but they are adequate and have good views of Ooty's tea fields.

The Fernhill offers two suites. The Maharaja Suite is furnished in blue and is awash with teak paneling and furniture. The lighter and brighter Maharani Suite also has its share of carved teak pieces. In addition, it boasts a patio overlooking a pleasantly shabby garden.

The Fernhill has facilities for squash, badminton, billiards, table tennis, and horse riding.

Ootacamund 643 004, South India. Tel. (0423) 3097. AE, DC,MC, V. Moderate. Monsoon and winter rates 50% of high season ones.

Kerala

CANNANORE

WYNAD

CALICUT

TRICHUR

IDUKKI

COCHIN

ALLEPPEY

PERIYAR

47 · PATHANAMTHITTA

QUILON

TRIVANDRUM

KOVALAM

Kerala

This sensuous state of palm trees, lagoons, and beaches is also one of India's most progressive regions. It is the state with the most educated population — 100% literacy rate for those under 30 — and the lowest birth rate in India. It is the state feisty enough to install the world's first freely elected communist government and cheeky enough to kick it out in the next poll. And it is the state where Christians, Jews, Arabs, and Muslims have always lived together harmoniously.

A sliver on India's west coast, the cosmopolitan Kerala has always opened its doors to foreign traders, who left their mark. Even St. Thomas is said to have preached in Kerala. Today the state is marked by India's oldest mosque, historical churches, and a unique synagogue in Kerala's largest city, **Cochin.**

But nature is as important here as history. You can putter through lagoons and canals in old boats, climb highlands with tea and spice plantations, and sun on one of India's best sandy beaches in **Kovalam.**

Kerala is also a center for ayurvedic medicine, the native healing system using cleansing, massage, and herbs to bring the body into balance. At Trivandrum's ayurvedic hospital you can see people testifying to cures by ayurveda after all avenues of Western medicine had failed.

Here prices are cheaper than in most of India, and the people more gentle and courteous. Thus far Kerala is one of India's undiscovered treasures. Visit it before it becomes overrun with tourists.

Cochin

The best thing about Cochin is its people. That is not to say that the city doesn't have things to see, but its educated citizens are some of the friendliest in India. Here you are hassled much less than in other places in the country and auto rickshaw drivers try to cheat you less often. There are even queues for buses instead of the mad stampede you encounter elsewhere.

This refreshing tone is due largely to Cochin's emphasis on education. In Cochin, and elsewhere in Kerala, there seem to be more people reading newspapers than there are beggars. The Kerala citizenry are informed and lively. Kerala's cultivated background comes in part from its long history as a trading center luring — and accepting — Chinese, Jews, Arabs, Portuguese, the British, and the Dutch. As Kerala's chief port city, Cochin has played a key role in its cosmopolitan hubbub. Here Chinese fishing nets stretch their graceful arms over the water, and a Jewish community still worships at a 500-year-old synagogue. Due to members leaving for Israel, the community has dwindled down to approximately 23 people, most of whom are elderly. As you wander through the overgrown cemetery, or visit the gleaming synagogue with treasures such as a 100-year-old Torah and blue and white tiles from China, you can almost hear the community's death knell.

Cochin also has India's oldest European-constructed church. **St. Francis Church** was built in 1503 by the Portuguese. Vasco da Gama was buried here briefly until his body was moved to Portugal. Also with a European heritage is the **Mattancherry,** or Dutch Palace. Although built by the Portuguese in 1557 for the maharaja, it was redone by the Dutch in 1663. It is now a museum with beautifully crafted murals depicting Indian gods. Some, such as one of the many-handed god Vishnu with every eager hand on the breast of a voluptuous maiden, are delightfully erotic.

But no visit to Cochin is complete without seeing a performance of the native dance **Kathakali**. Originally designed to last for many hours at temple performances, Kathakali has been shortened for modern tastes. It is performed by only a drummer, singer, and dancers. Dancers tell religious stories by activating what seems to be every muscle in their bodies. Facial expressions are as important here as leg and arm movements. Also fascinating are their costumes and elaborately painted faces, which contribute to the dance's meaning.

Bolgatty Palace Hotel

At first glance the Bolgatty Palace is a bit, ahem, shabby. The lovely old teak floors and furniture haven't seen much care. Public areas with their motley assemblage of fleamarket-genre odds and ends need a decorator's hand. But be forewarned. This rangy old building grows on you. Maybe it's the many windows and the restaurant patio that make you feel as if you are in a tropical paradise. Maybe it's the coziness of watching from your room with its wall of windows as a fierce monsoon rain lashes the building. Or it could be the waterfront location, and the 16 acres of semi-wild gardens and grasslands that surround the hotel, so that nature always seems present here.

Part of the romance of the Bolgatty is that it's on its own island and can only be reached by boat, which leaves frequently from the High Court jetty across the way. Although a frequent stop of tour groups, it never seems overrun. Especially at night, life on the island shuts down except for the sleepy palace hotel, leaving the wild and wicked city lights of Cochin twinkling across the water.

The hotel was built in 1744 by the Dutch as an outpost for their army commanders. From 1804 until Indian independence it was the British residency. In its next phase the palace was used as a guest house for government VIPs until 1976, when it was made into a hotel. It is presently run by the government's Kerala Tourist Development Corp.

In 1981 the KTDC added six cottages that are scattered throughout the hotel grounds. They are among India's tackiest accommodations. Avoid them.

Although genteelly decaying, the five spacious standard rooms in the old building have a historic feeling about them. They lack air conditioning, however, but that is not a problem in the winter and monsoon seasons.

The hotel includes both a restaurant and bar. Because KTDC employees can't be fired, expect service to range from professional to sloppy.

Mulavukadu P. O., Cochin 682 504, Kerala, India. Tel. 355003,353234. AE, DC, MC. 50% off in June, July. Inexpensive.

Periyar Wildlife Sanctuary

In the cool highlands, the 777 sq km of the Periyar Wildlife Sanctuary in the small southwestern state of Kerala is one of the best places to see wild elephants in India. Some 800 elephants live here. Best time to see them is during the dry months between October and April when they come to the lake to drink. They are relaxed around humans, allowing closeup looks from boats.

Their lake is an artificial one created a century ago by damming the Periyar River. A few naked tree trunks from the forest that was submerged when the lake was formed still poke up forlornly from the water.

Along with elephants, you can see wild oxen, or gaur, deer, wild pig, and many species of birds here. Periyar also has tigers, but the shy beast is rarely spotted. Best wildlife viewing is from the lake. Animals seem to have grown accustomed to curious humans watching them from the water. The Kerala Tourist Department operates frequent launches from the Aranya Nivas Hotel, but these are often full of noisy tourists. Best bet is to rent your own boat from the Aranya Nivas.

Lake Palace

There are no stuffed dead animal trophies at the Lake Palace. The maharaja of Travancore, who built the palace in 1936, was forward-looking both politically and ecologically. He spent less money on himself than other Indian maharajas, funneling his funds into projects to help his people. He also was not a hunter and preferred to appreciate animals rather than kill them.

The Lake Palace was his back-to-nature lodge. Members of the royal family used to pile into the royal launch to make the trek to the Lake Palace, which is located on its own island in the middle of Periyar's lake. Men were clad in the native skirt, the *lunghi,* and women wore sarongs with blouses and much jewelry. The lifestyles of the Kerala royals were much simpler than those of their northern cousins. Their lodge also is more basic than those found in the north. Made with native stone, it is in the Kerala style with peaked shiny roof.

Rooms 11 and 22 and the dining room compose the original building. In 1980 the hotel added a new wing. Today the lodge combines both old and new decor. The dining room has nice old tables and chairs. A few pieces of palace teak furniture such as old coat racks grace most of the six rooms. Rooms 55, 33, 11, and 22 sport the delightful v-shaped Keralan ceiling. Rooms 66 and 44 have lake views.

The Lake Palace affords the best glimpses of wildlife in Periyar. There is a terrace on which you can sit and view the animals on the shore. In between animal times you can wander around the hotel's beautiful gardens.

Aranya Nivas Hotel, Thekkady 685 536, Kerala, India. Tel. Kumily 23. Telegrams ARANYANIVAS. AE, DC, MC, V. Expensive.

ADDITIONAL READING
Other travel books from Hunter Publishing:

INSIDER'S GUIDE TO INDIA
What to see and do, how to get around, where to eat, where to stay, region by region, along with extensive historical and cultural background on the country. Hundreds of color photos and maps. Includes large fold-out map. Available in the UK through Moorland Publishing. **360 pp paperback/6 x 9/$16.95/ISBN 1-55650-164-1**

INDIA
Part of the Times Travel Library, here is one of the most lavish color paperbacks ever produced. Filled with maps and practical information, but the spectacular color photos are what set this guide apart. **96 pp paperback/7 x 10/$14.95/ISBN 1-55650-259-1**

INDIA/NEPAL (HILDEBRAND TRAVEL GUIDE)
Striking color photos, concise fact-packed writing, complete practical information as well as chapters on the food, society, and culture of India. Includes small fold-out map. **224 pp paperback/4 x 6/$11.95/ISBN 3-88989-075-X**

INDIA BY RAIL
The ideal way to see the country. Everything is here, from how to plan your trip, booking, and comfort on board to suggested itineraries and scenic routes. Available in the UK through Bradt Publications. **204 pp paperback/5 x 8/$16.95/1-55650-187-0**

INDIA (HILDEBRAND TRAVEL MAP)
The best large folding map of the country. Full color, with index. 1:4,255,000 scale. Includes city maps of the major towns as well. Approximately 4 x 5 feet unfolded. **$8.95/ISBN 3-88989-238-8**

INSIDER'S GUIDE TO NEPAL
Spectacular color photos on every page, with color maps and a text that covers all practical details for the traveller. Special sections examine the country's amazing history and culture. Large fold-out map included. (UK: Moorland Publishing) **224 pp paperback/6 x 9/$17.95/ISBN 1-55650-185-4**

VIDEO VISITS

Focussing on the timeless aspects of each destination, the unique sights, history, and culture, these 50-minute videos capture the beauty and grandeur of the world's great cities and countries. Winners of top honors for their entertainment and information value: ITA Golden Video Award; CINE Golden Eagle Award; ITA Platinum Video Award; Gold Medal, NY International Film Festival. **$29.95 each.** There are over 70 titles in the series, including:

AUSTRALIA
BALI
CHINA/TIBET/HONG KONG/MACAU
INDIA
JAPAN
MALAYSIA
NEW ZEALAND
MOSCOW/ST PETERSBURG
SINGAPORE
TAIWAN
THAILAND

CHARMING SMALL HOTELS

This series describes the hotels we all dream of discovering, the special places that combine individuality, atmosphere, service, good food and good value. Each guide contains hundreds of up-to-date on-site inspections of the hotels by a team of discerning travel writers. 300 or more hotels are profiled in each guide, with color photos throughout. **224 pp paperbacks/4 x 8/$12.95.** Titles include:

BRITAIN & IRELAND 1-55650-065-3
FRANCE 1-55650-468-3
GERMANY 1-55650-502-7
ITALY 1-55650-467-5
SPAIN 1-55650-285-2

ADVENTURE TRAVEL

Illustrated in color, with numerous maps, these comprehensive guidebooks cover all practical information a traveller will need, with an emphasis on exploring off the beaten track. Extensive background sections cover history and social structure. All are 5 x 8 paperbacks.

ADVENTURE GUIDE TO THE ALASKA HIGHWAY 288 pp/$15.95/1-55650-457-8

ADVENTURE GUIDE TO BAJA 320 pp/$15.95/1-55650-251-6

ADVENTURE GUIDE TO BARBADOS 224 pp/$16.95/1-55650- 277-X

ADVENTURE GUIDE TO BELIZE 288 pp/$15.95/1-55650-493-4

ADVENTURE GUIDE TO CANADA 320 pp/$16.95/1-55650-315-6

ADVENTURE GUIDE TO COSTA RICA 448 pp/$16.95/1-55650-456-X

ADVENTURE GUIDE TO THE EVERGLADES & FLORIDA KEYS 224 pp/$14.95/1-55650-494-2

ADVENTURE GUIDE TO JAMAICA 288 pp/$17.95/1-55650-499-3

ADVENTURE GUIDE TO PUERTO RICO 224 pp/$15.95/1-55650-178-1

ADVENTURE GUIDE TO THE SOUTH PACIFIC 448 pp/$16.95/1-55650-108-0

ADVENTURE GUIDE TO THE VIRGIN ISLANDS 208 pp/$15.95/1-55650-500-0

HAWAII: A WALKER'S GUIDE 224 pp/$14.95/1-55650-215-X

Write Hunter Publishing, 300 Raritan Center Parkway, Edison NJ 08818 or call (908) 225 1900 for our free color catalog describing these and hundreds of other unusual travel guides, maps and travel videos to virtually every destination on earth. All can be found in the best bookstores or you can order direct from the address above (please add $2.50 to cover shipping/handling).